アールヌーボーの花々が歌うキルト

リバティの詩
POEMS OF LIBERTY

Quilts Echoing the Flowers of Art Nouveau

POEMS OF LIBERTY
2 BED COVER

First edition Dec. 10, 1994
Copyright   ©1994 by Himeko Nakanishi
Text by Haruhiko Fujita
Edited by Kimi Himeno
Photographs by Studio Kanno
Translated by Kimiko Steiner
Designed by Asako Nambu
Published by Kyoto Shoin Co., LTD.
Sanjo-agaru, Horikawa, Nakagyo-ku, Kyoto, 604 Japan

ISBN4-7636-3243-4

All rights reserved. No part of this book may be reproduced or transmitted
in any form or by any means without permission in writing from the publisher.

Printed in Japan by Taihei Printing Co., Ltd.

CONTENTS

ベッドカバー　中西一女子
Bedcover　by Himeko NAKANISHI
4

作品
Collections
9

リバティ・スタイルとフリー・スタイル　藤田治彦
Liberty Style and Free Style　by Haruhiko FUJITA
88

作品リスト
List
95

　　　　　　　　　私は、新しい布に出会うと
　　　まず10cmの正方形に切りとって眺めてみるくせがあります。
　　そして、気に入った柄は、アトリエの壁に貼りつけておきます。
リバティの布はこのくらいの大きさだと、デザインされた模様がそのまま保存され、
　　　　美しいものを切り刻んでしまう不安から救われるのです。
また、真四角という形自体がもつふくらみとぬくもりにも親しみを覚えるのです。

でも、どうやってそれらの様々な表情の布たちを共生させることができるのでしょうか。
　　　　　　悩んだあげく、私は簡単な結論を出しました。
　　　──自分の好きな柄を、10cm四方のそのままの形でみんな集合させて、
　　　　　　　　大きなベッドカバーにしてしまおう──
　　　　「リバティ・パレード」と名付けた第一作はこうして生まれました。
　　リバティの本店がある、あの美しいカーヴを描いたリージェント・ストリートを
　　私の号令のもとに勢ぞろいした布たちが行進していくというイメージです。
　　　手に取ってみると、一つ一つのお気に入りの模様が楽しめますし、
離れて全体を見ると、私だけのものという創作の充実感を少しは味わえるのでした。

それから後、私はもうためらいなしに布たちを切って並べることができるようになりました。
　　　　　　　　　「紅いダイヤモンドダスト」は、
　　　オックスフォードのある寒い朝にみた自然の造形から思いついたもの。
　　　　　　　　「アンドロメダ星雲の夜明け」は、
　　　本で読んだ大宇宙の物語から勝手に空想したもの……です。

もちろん旅の想い出も大きな刺激です。
なかでも私が一番強い感動を覚えたのは、アルハンブラ宮殿の内陣です。
アラブ人の支配から独立を取り戻したばかりのスペインの王様が、
こだわりなく、アラブの職人たちに存分の腕をふるわせた雅量の大きさもさることながら
それに応えてつくられたモザイクタイルの模様の美しさは何と言ったらいいのでしょう。
部分部分をみると、ごく単純な四角や三角でしかないのに、
全体の構成、そのバランスと色調の天国のような神々しさ……。
名もない人々が淡々と積み重ねていったその仕事、職人芸の限りない深さに心をうたれます。
私など、もちろん及びもつかない世界ですが、
「アルハンブラの思い出」は、そんな感動に突き動かされて作ったのでした——。

ベッドカバー
by Himeko Nakanishi

I have a habit that whenever I encounter a new piece of cloth,
I cut out 10 by 10 cm squares and admire them.
Those patterns which please me, I affix to the wall of my studio.
Using such a size for the Liberty cloth
allows the designed patterns to be preserved in full,
saving me from the anxiety of cutting up something beautiful.
I feel a further attachment to the fullness and
warmth of the square itself.

However, the question remained:
how was I to arrange the pieces of cloth,
with their various powers of expressions,
into a harmonious interplay?
After much deliberation, I came to a simple conclusion.
Gathering the 10 by 10 cm pieces of cloth as they were,
I chose to assemble them into one large bedcover....
It was thus that my first piece, "Liberty Parade," was born.
As an image, I pictured the pieces of cloth
marching in line to my commands,
down the beautifully curved Regent Street,
home to the main Liberty shop.
Taking the cover in hand, I was able to enjoy
each of my favorite patterns individually;
and witnessing the entire work from a distance,
I was able to savor a sense of fulfillment from my creation,
knowing that it was all my own.

*After that, I became able to cut and arrange pieces of cloth
without the slightest hesitation.
"Crimson Diamond Dust" came to me from the natural forms
I witnessed on a chilly morning in Oxford.
"Dawn of Andromeda" was a flight of fancy inspired by
a story set in space which I read in a book.
Of course, memories of travel provide
a great stimulus to my work.
Of all of these, that which moved me the most was
the inside of the Alhambra Palace.
Having just restored independence from Arab rule,
the king of Spain abandoned his preconceptions
and gave full play to the skills of Arab artisans.
Such magnanimity being as it may, the resulting beauty
of the mosaic tilework produced there defies description.
Each individual part is a simple rectangle or triangle;
yet the whole, with its composition, balance
and heavenly color tone...
One is moved by the limitless depth of artistry,
the steady yet serene work of these nameless men.
It is, of course, a world totally beyond my reach,
but it moved me to create my piece, "Memory of Alhambra."*

Bedcover

by Himeko Nakanishi

BED COVER

made with

LIBERTY

1 アルハンブラの思い出／Memory of Alhambra

2 アルハンブラの思い出／Memory of Alhambra

11

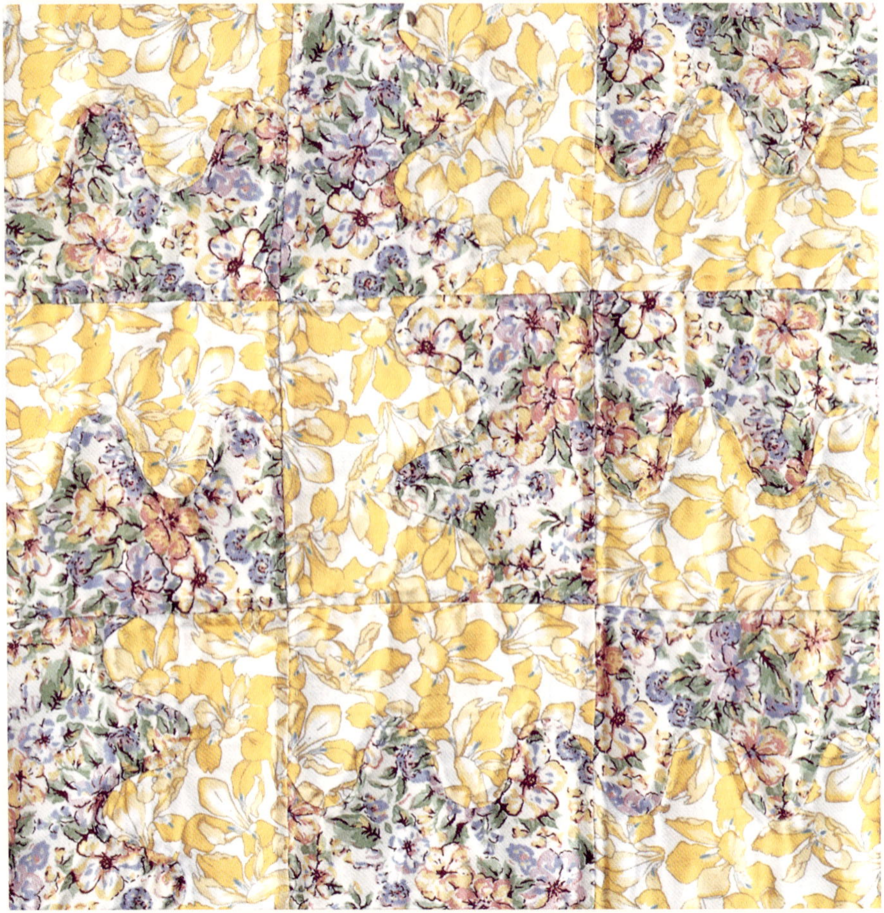

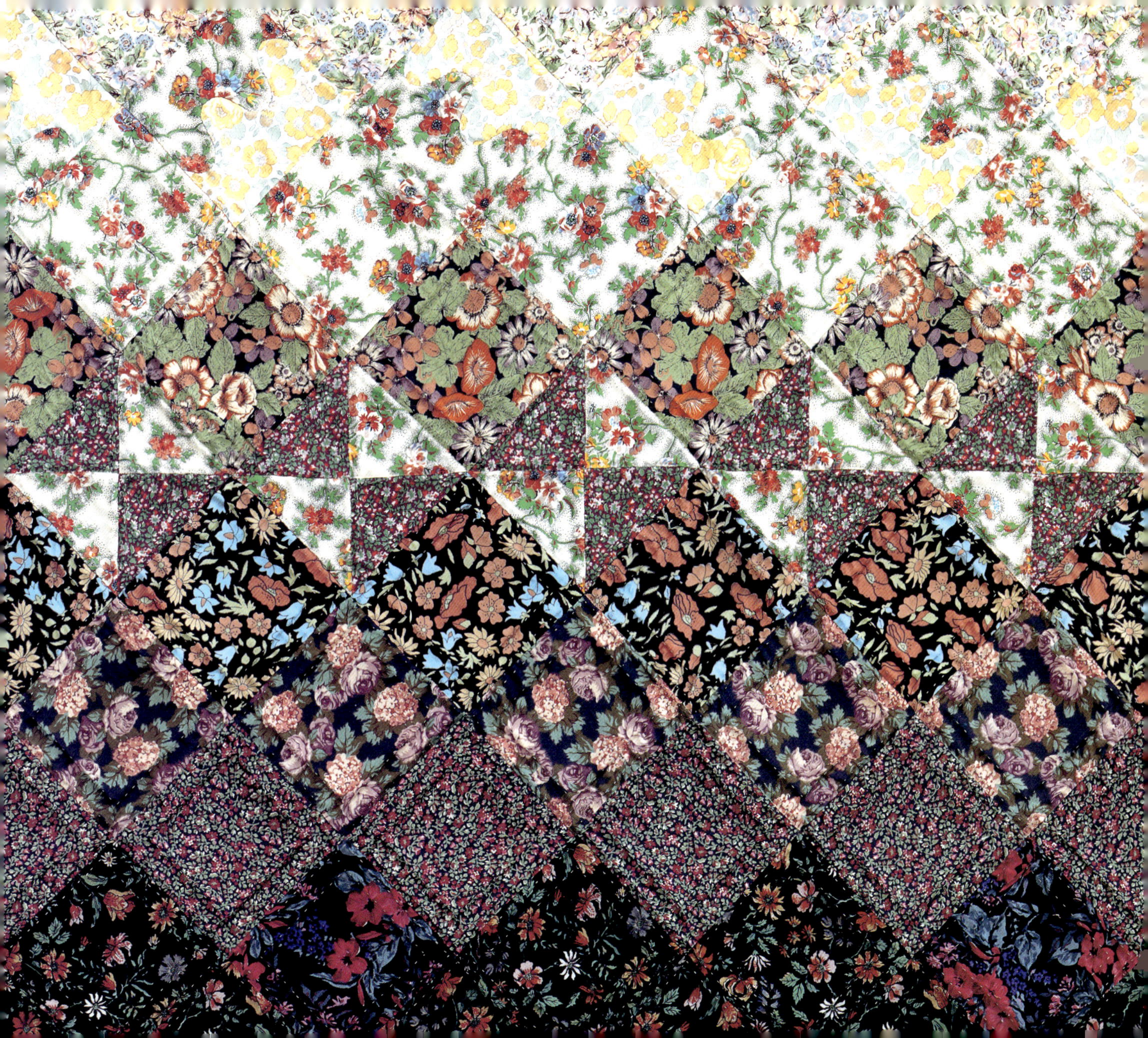

14

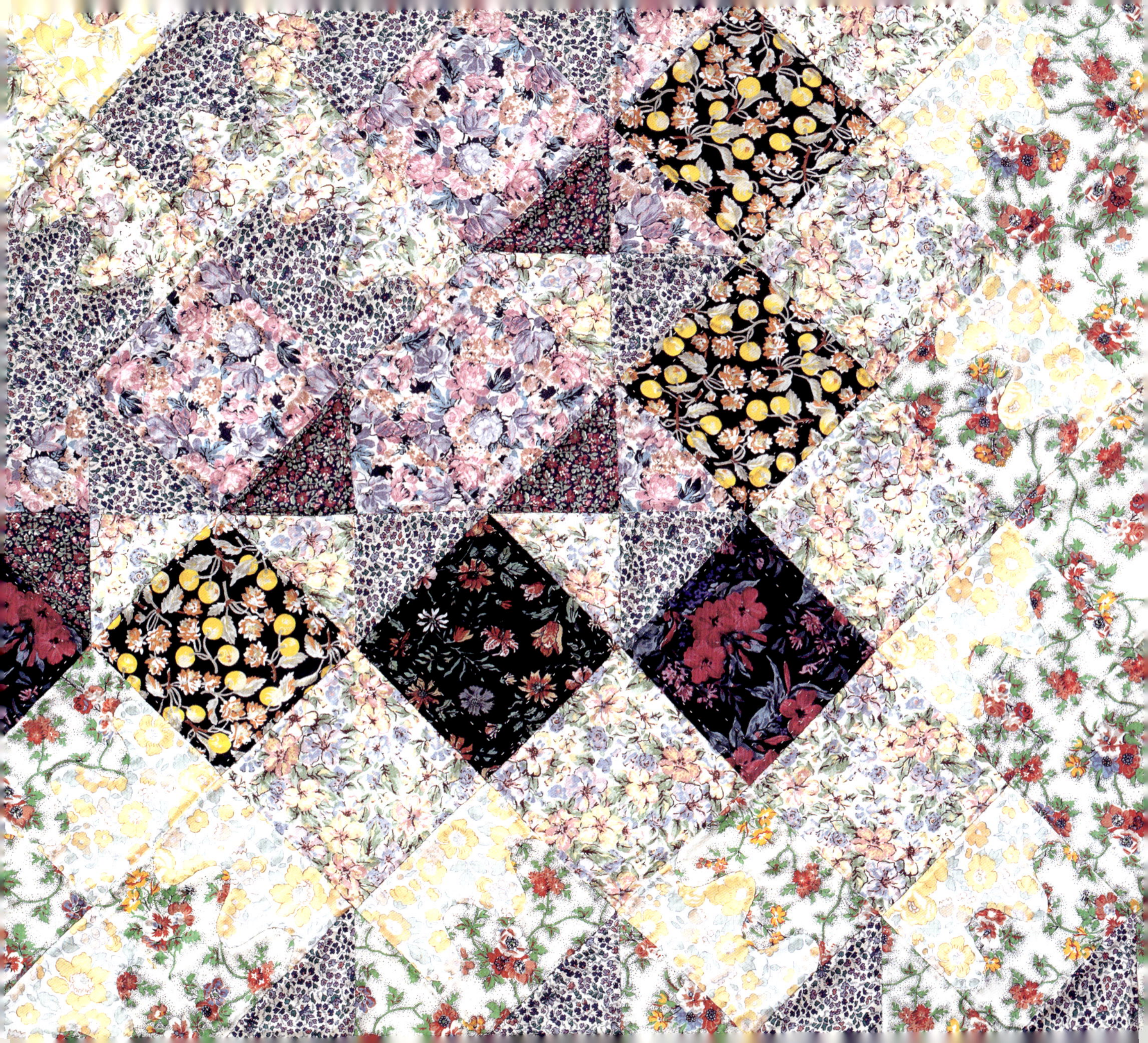

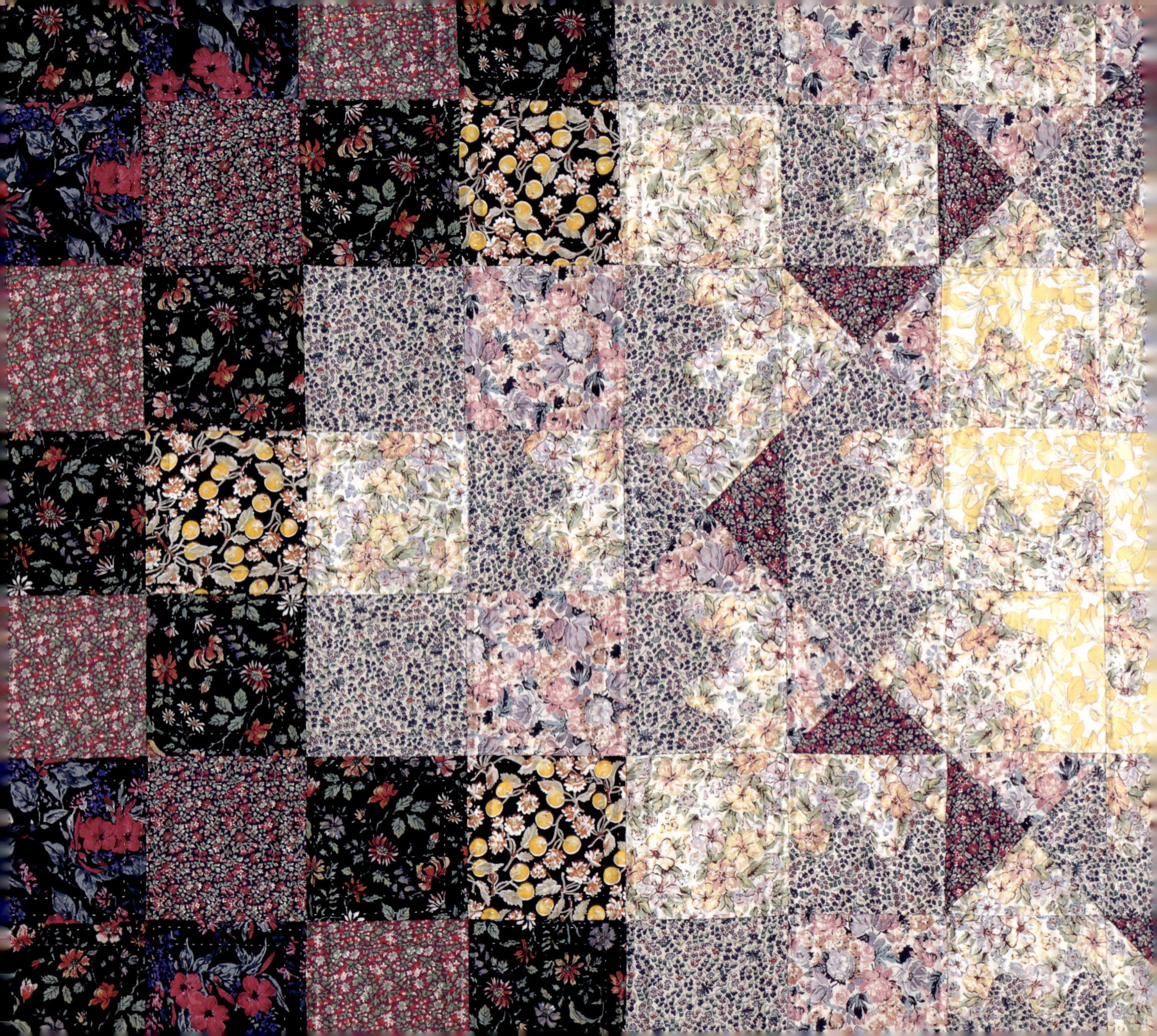

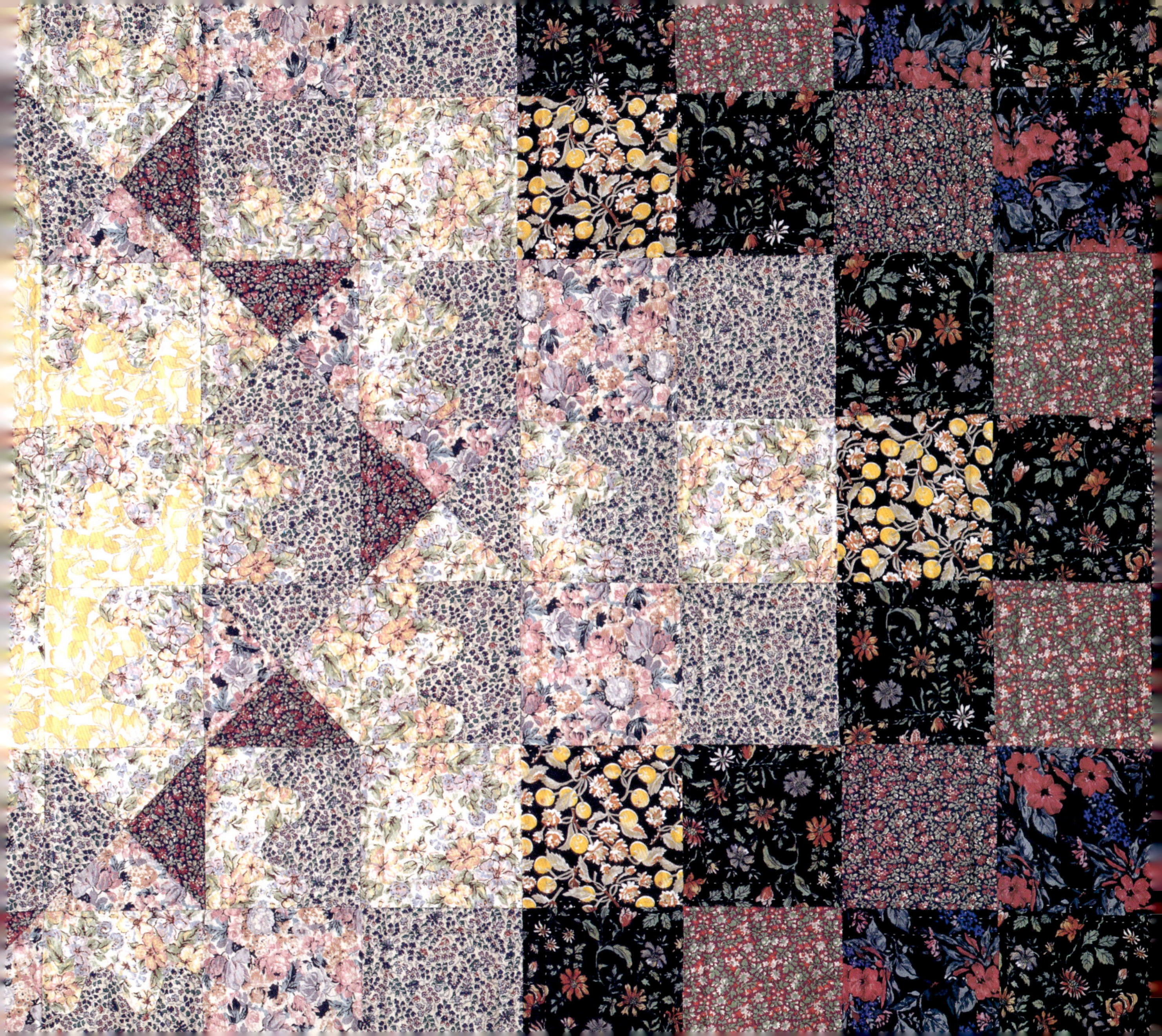

3 プロヴァンスのキルト／Provençal Quilt

19

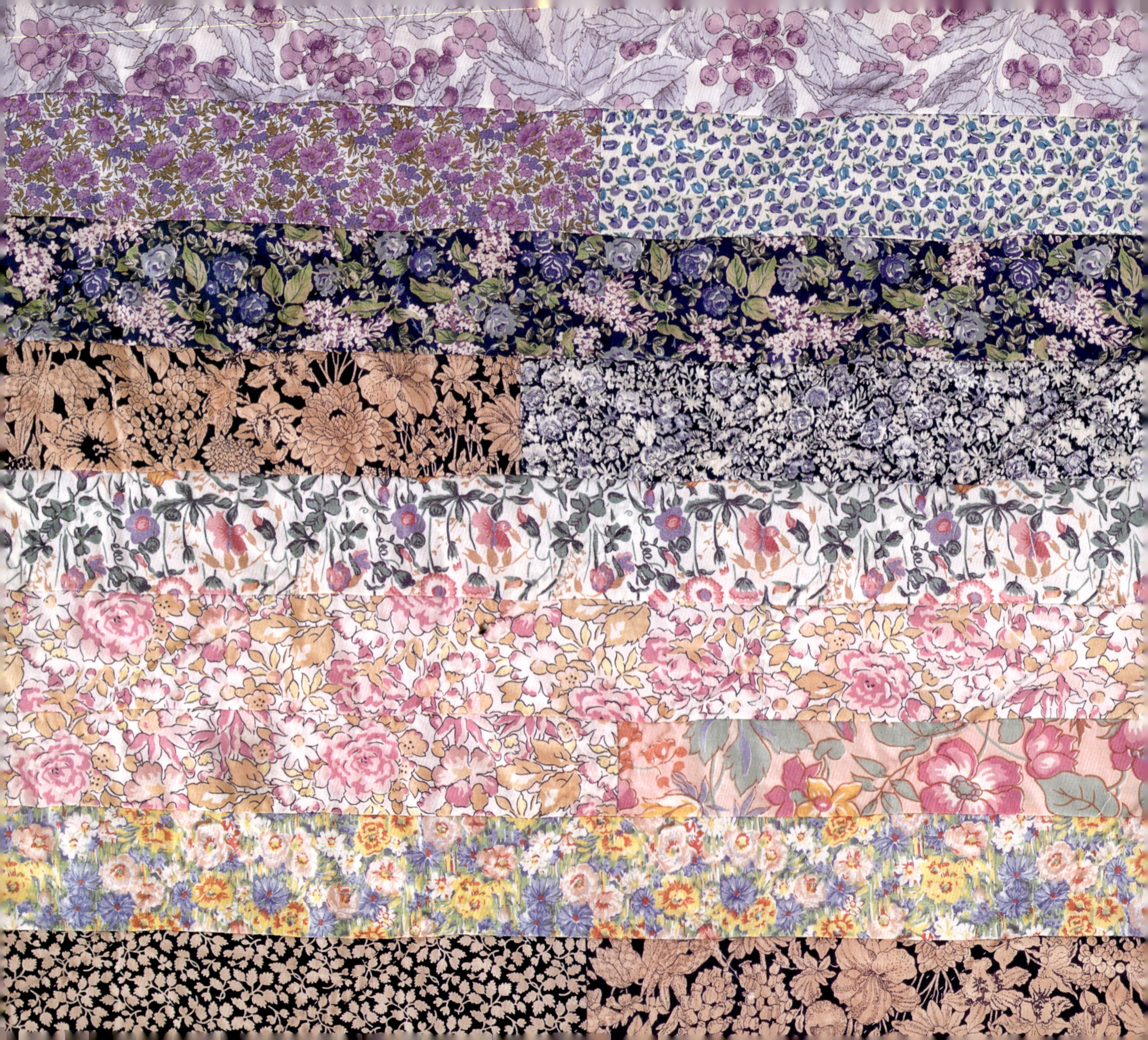

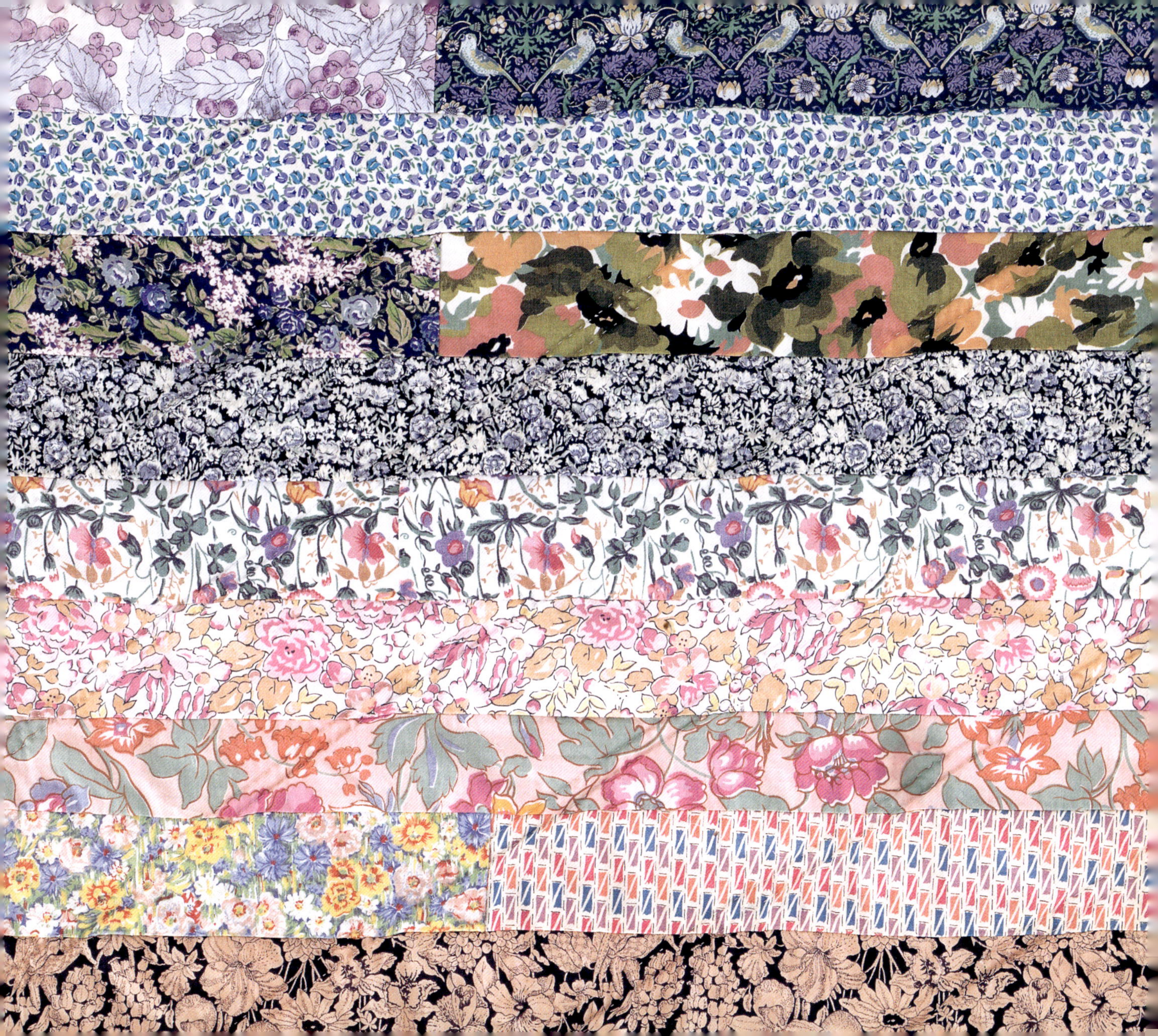

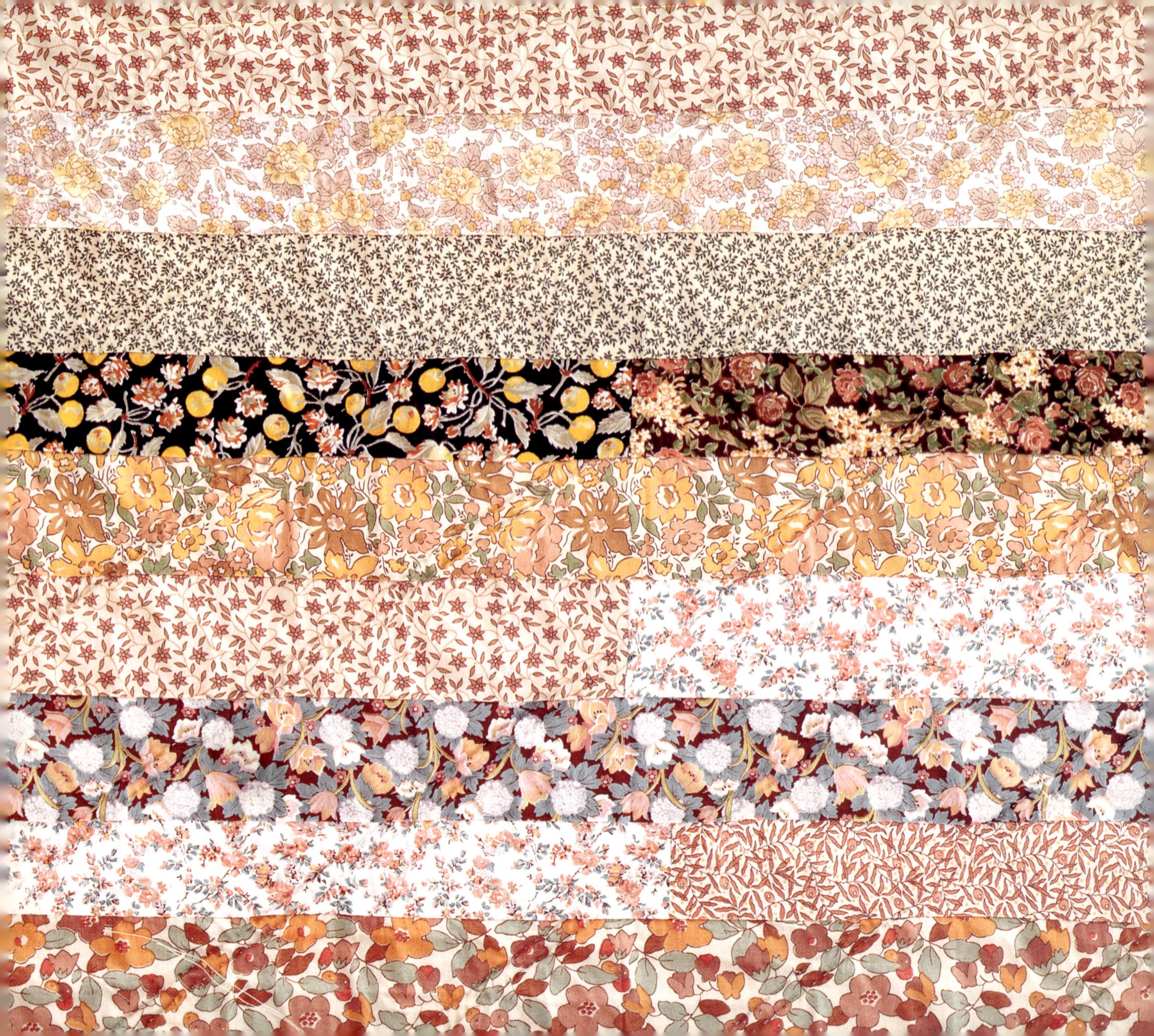

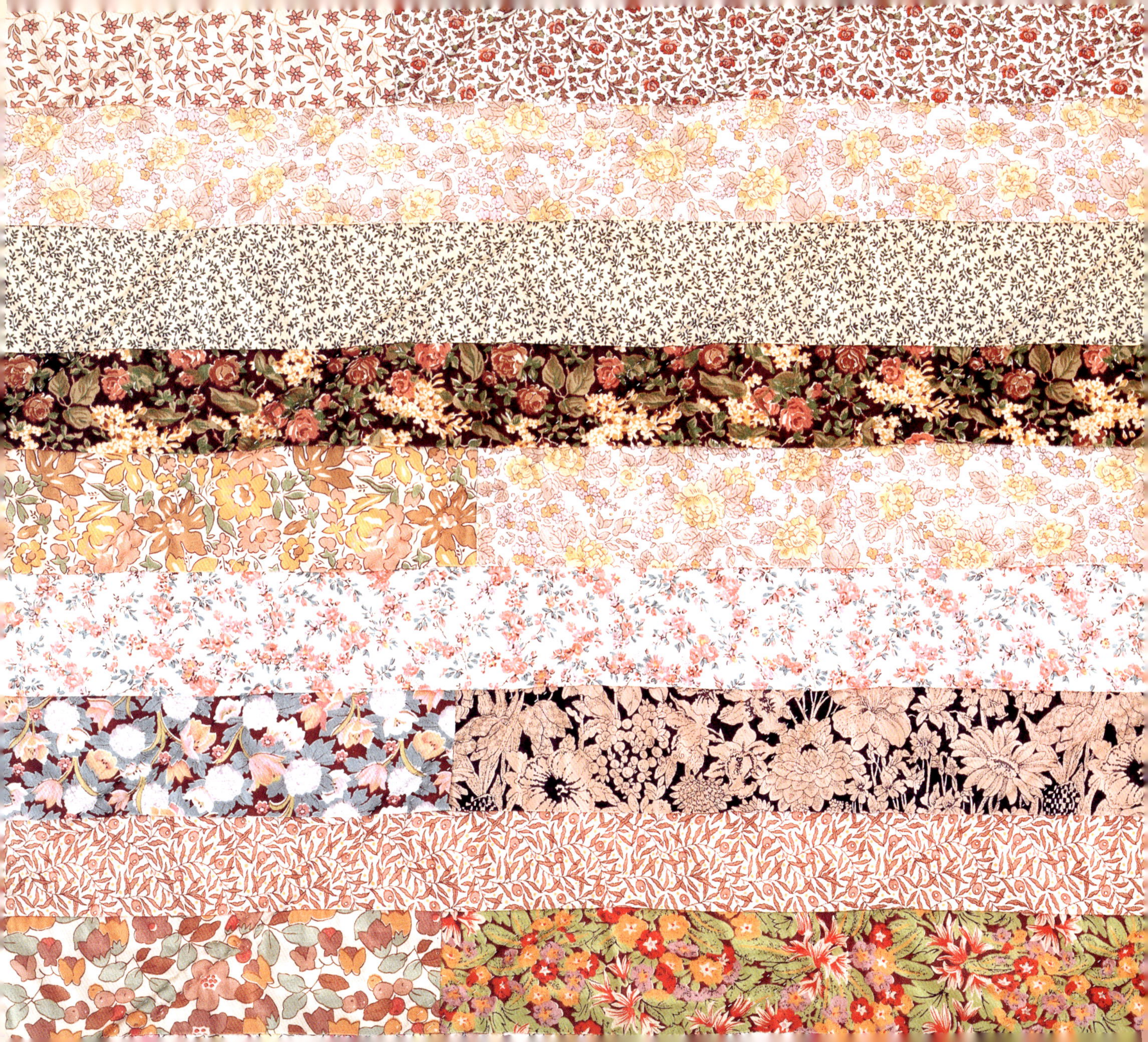

4 パイルドキルト／Piled Quilt

25

5 パイルドキルト／Piled Quilt

27

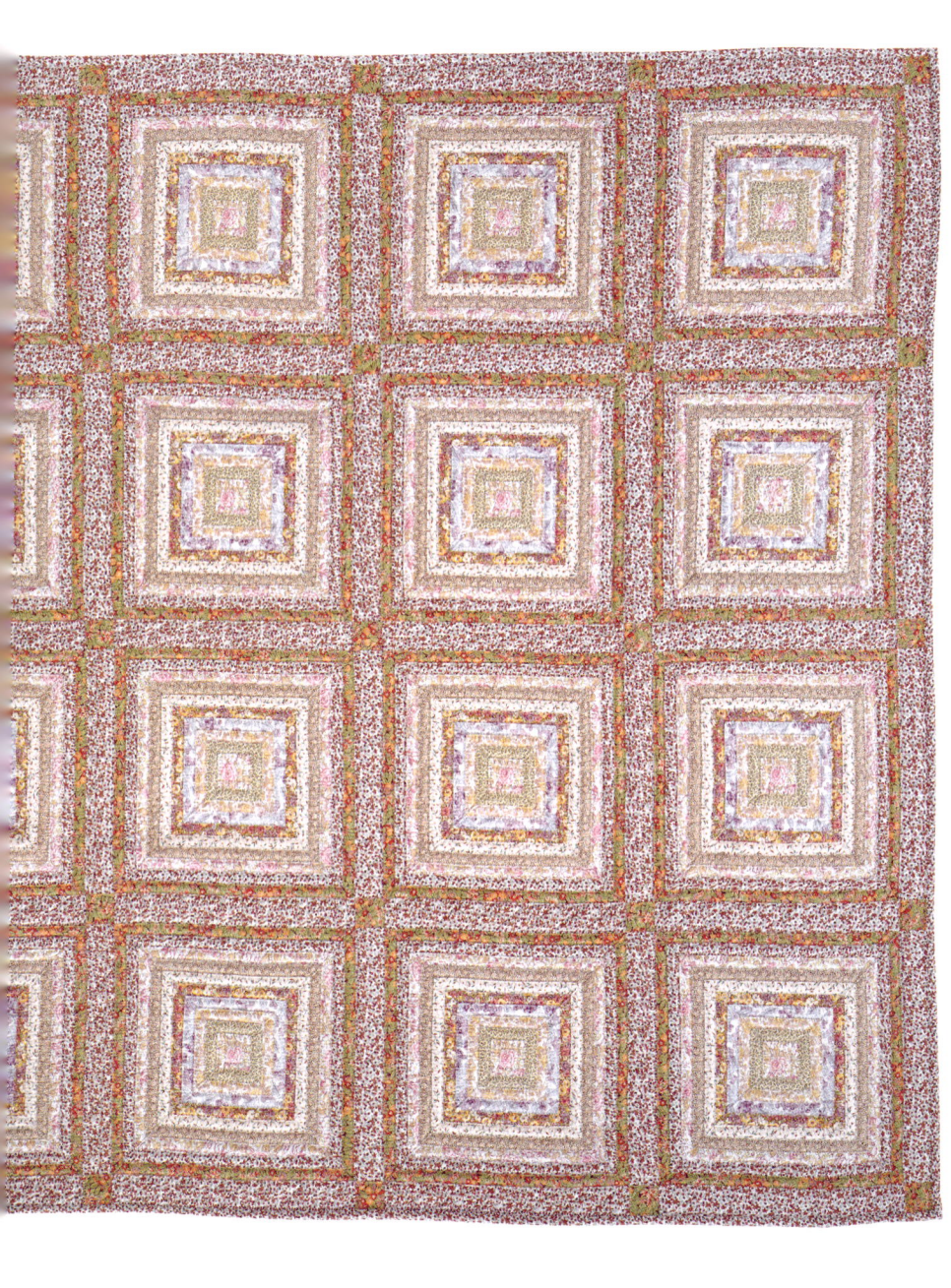

28

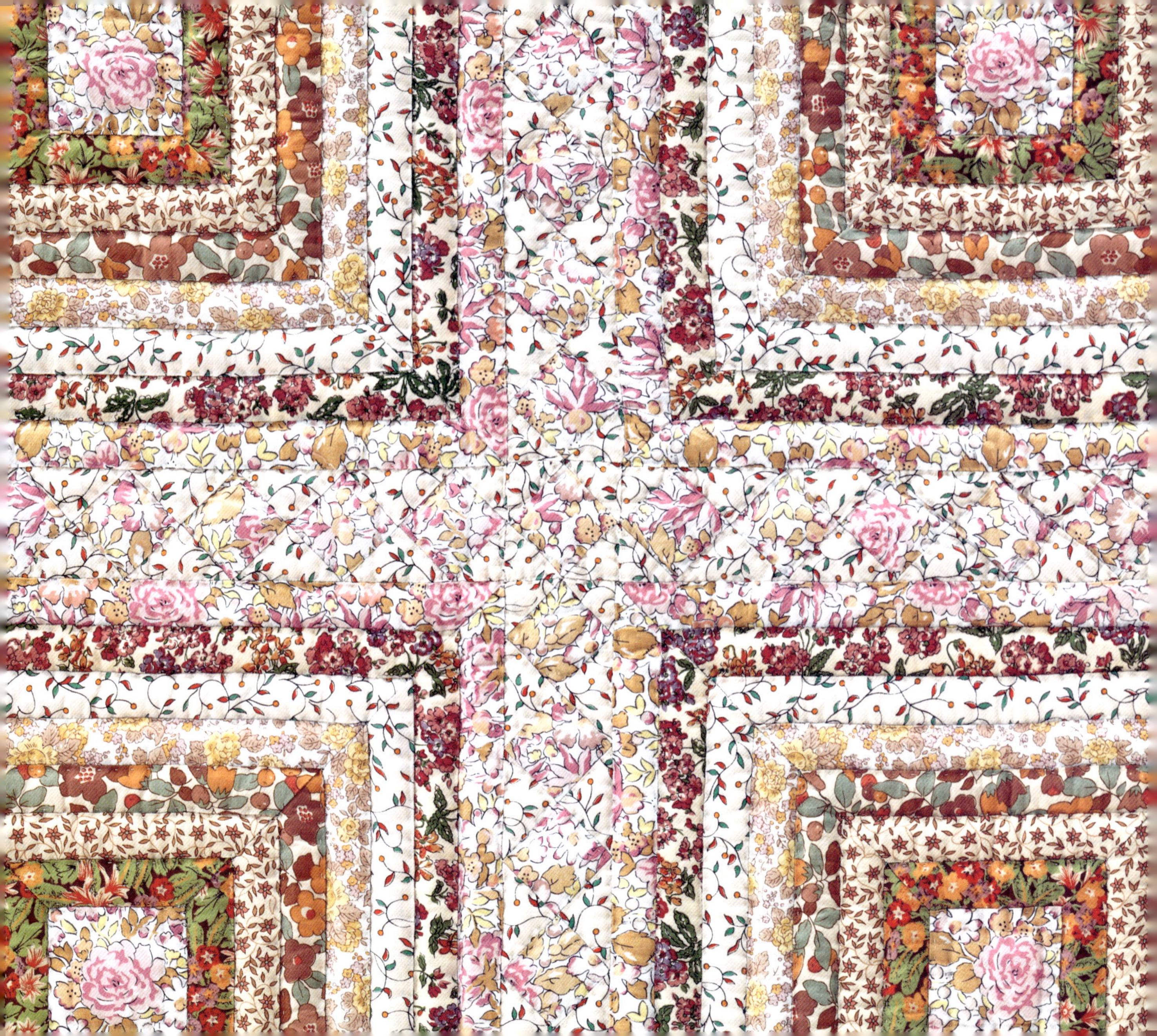

6 アンドロメダ星雲の夜明け／Dawn of Andromeda

31

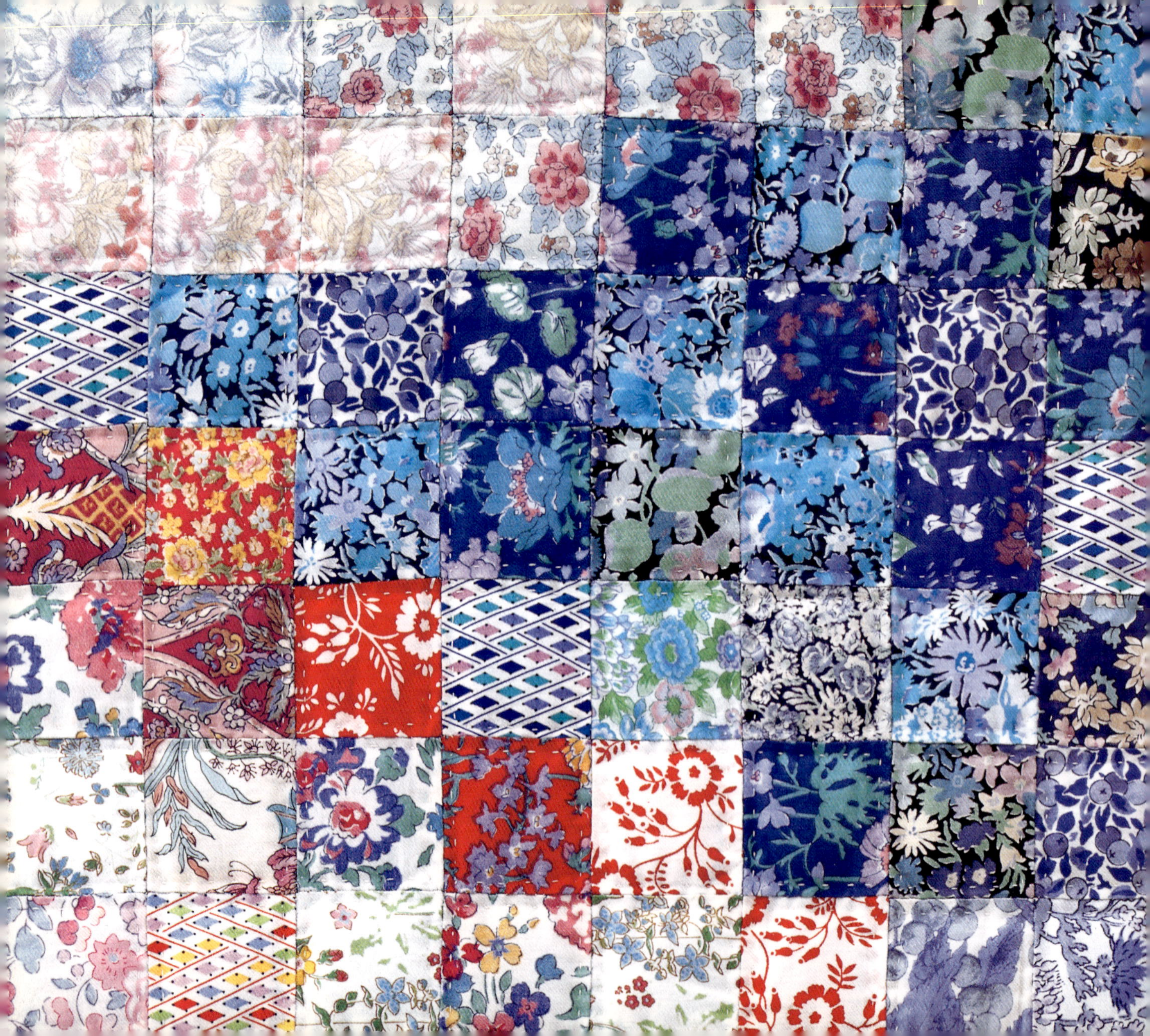

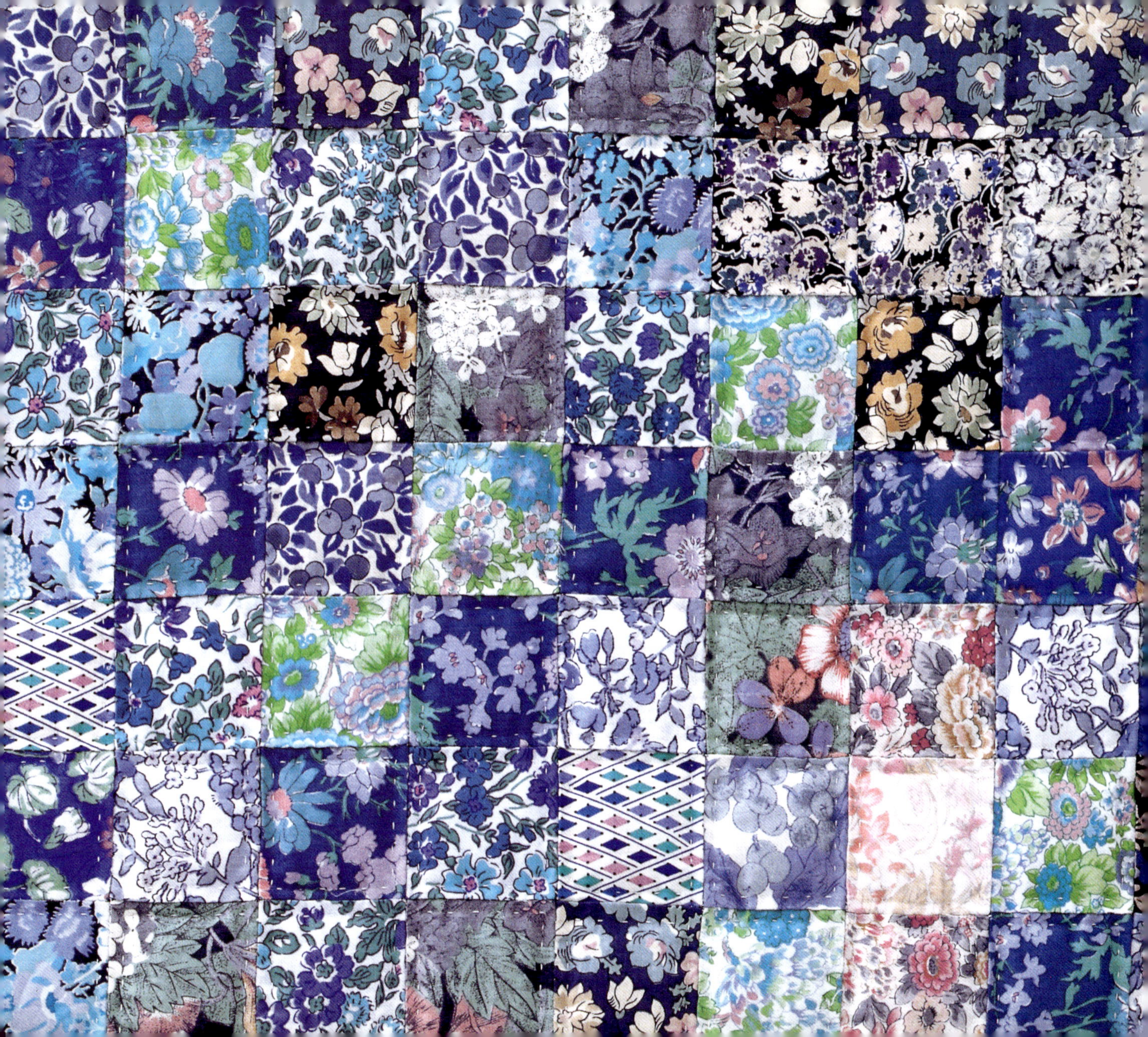

7 モノクローム・モザイク／Monochromic Mosaic

35

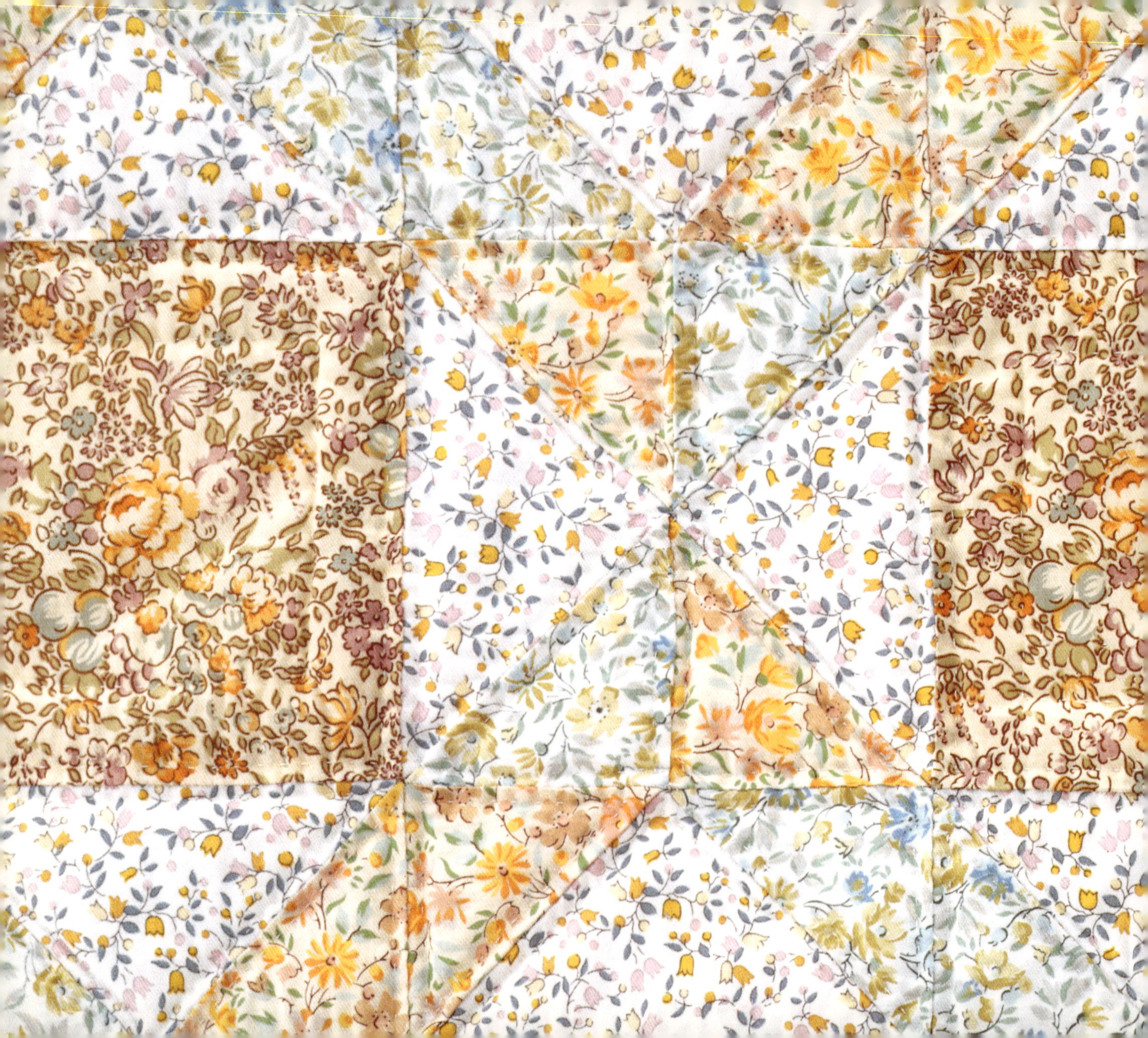

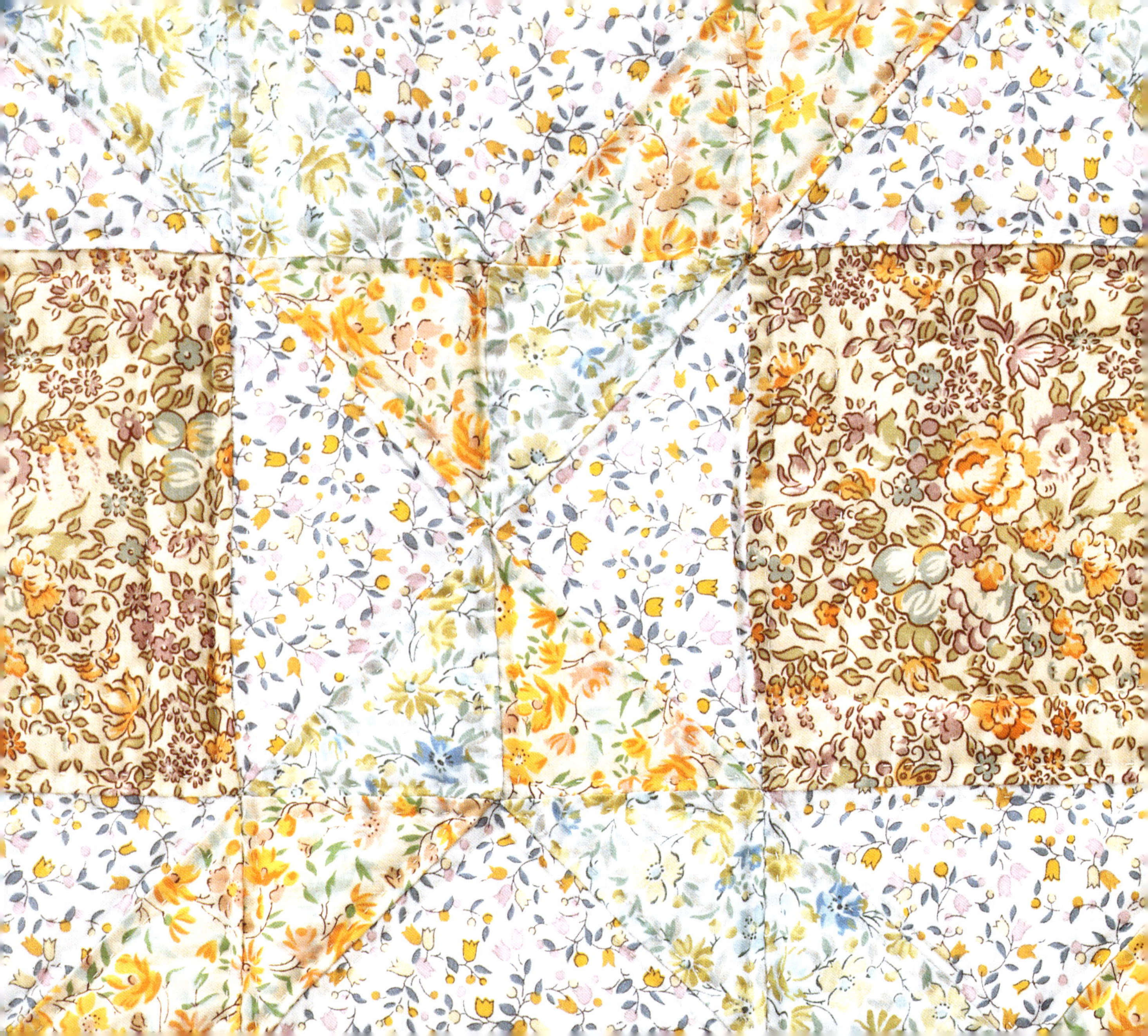

38

8 ベルサイユの庭／Garden of Versailles

40

41

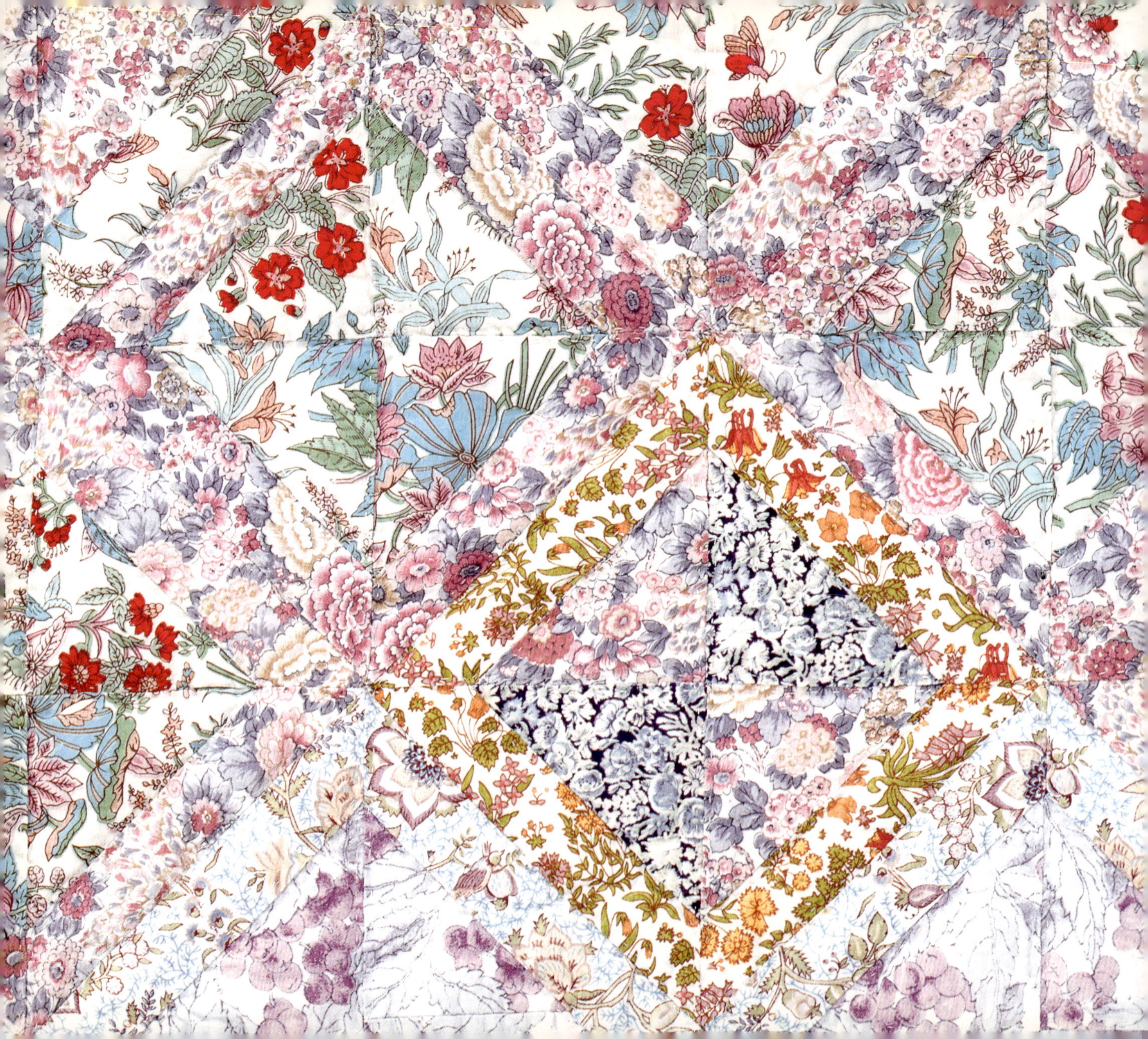

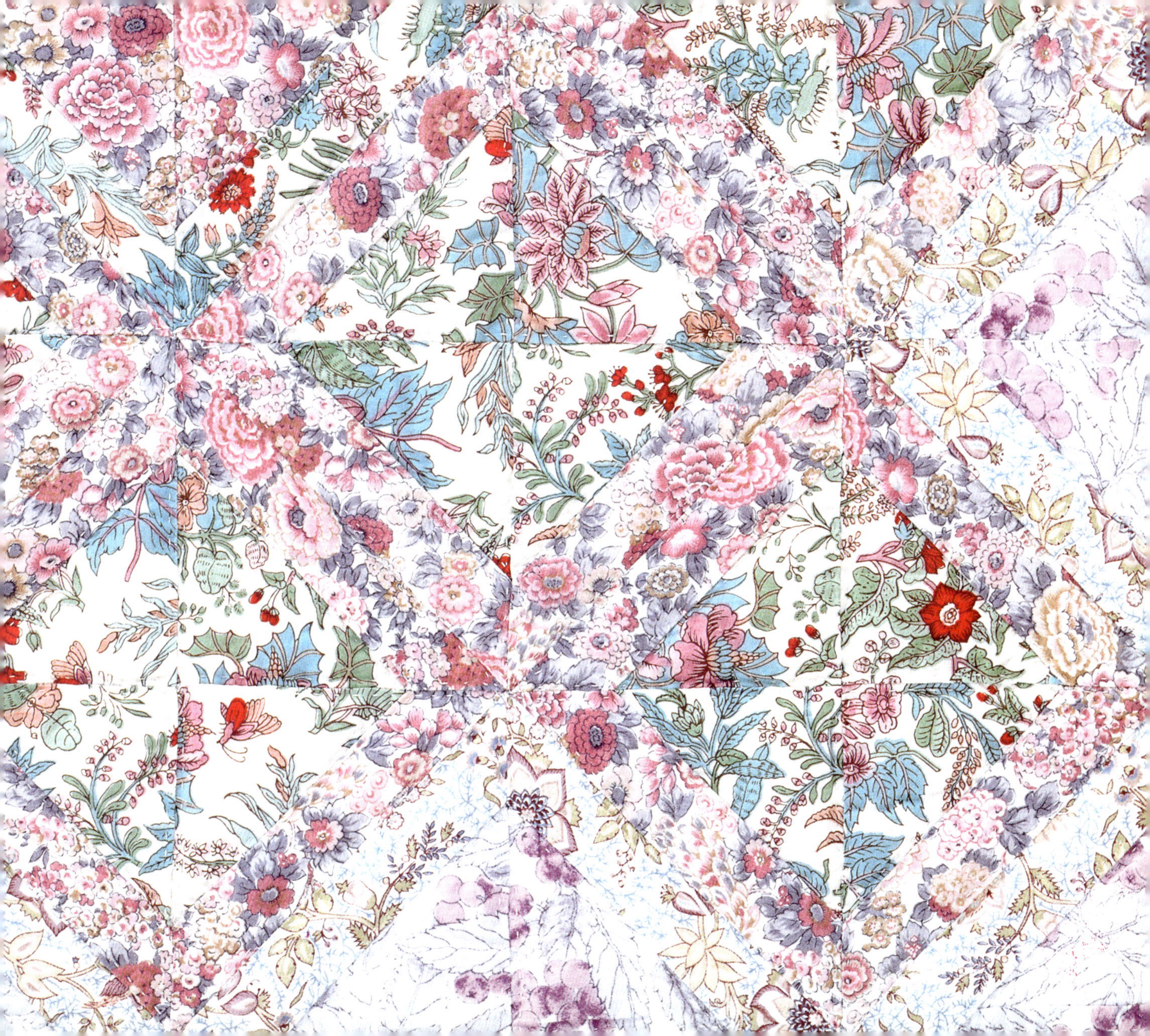

44

9　イギリスの庭／Old England Garden

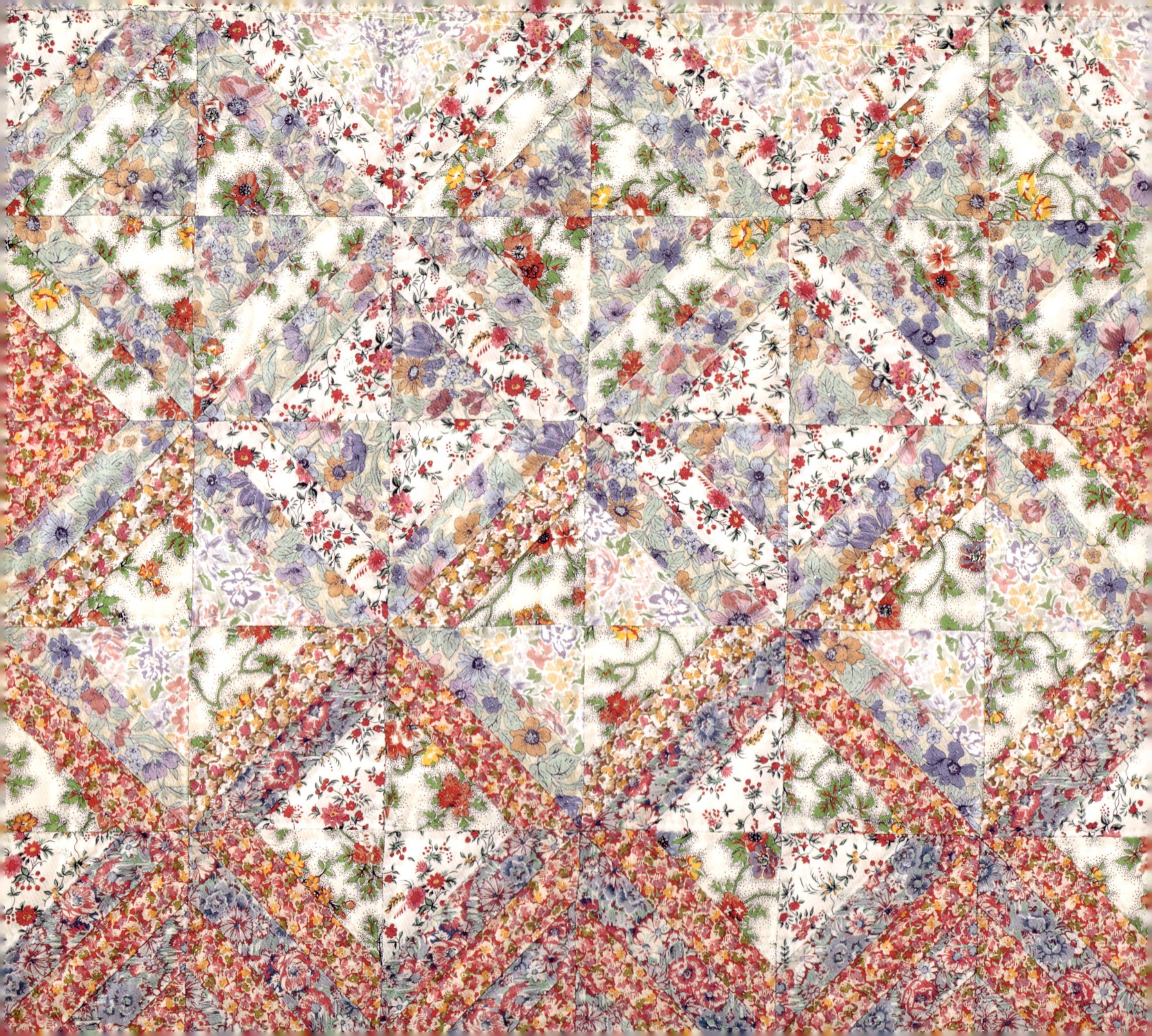

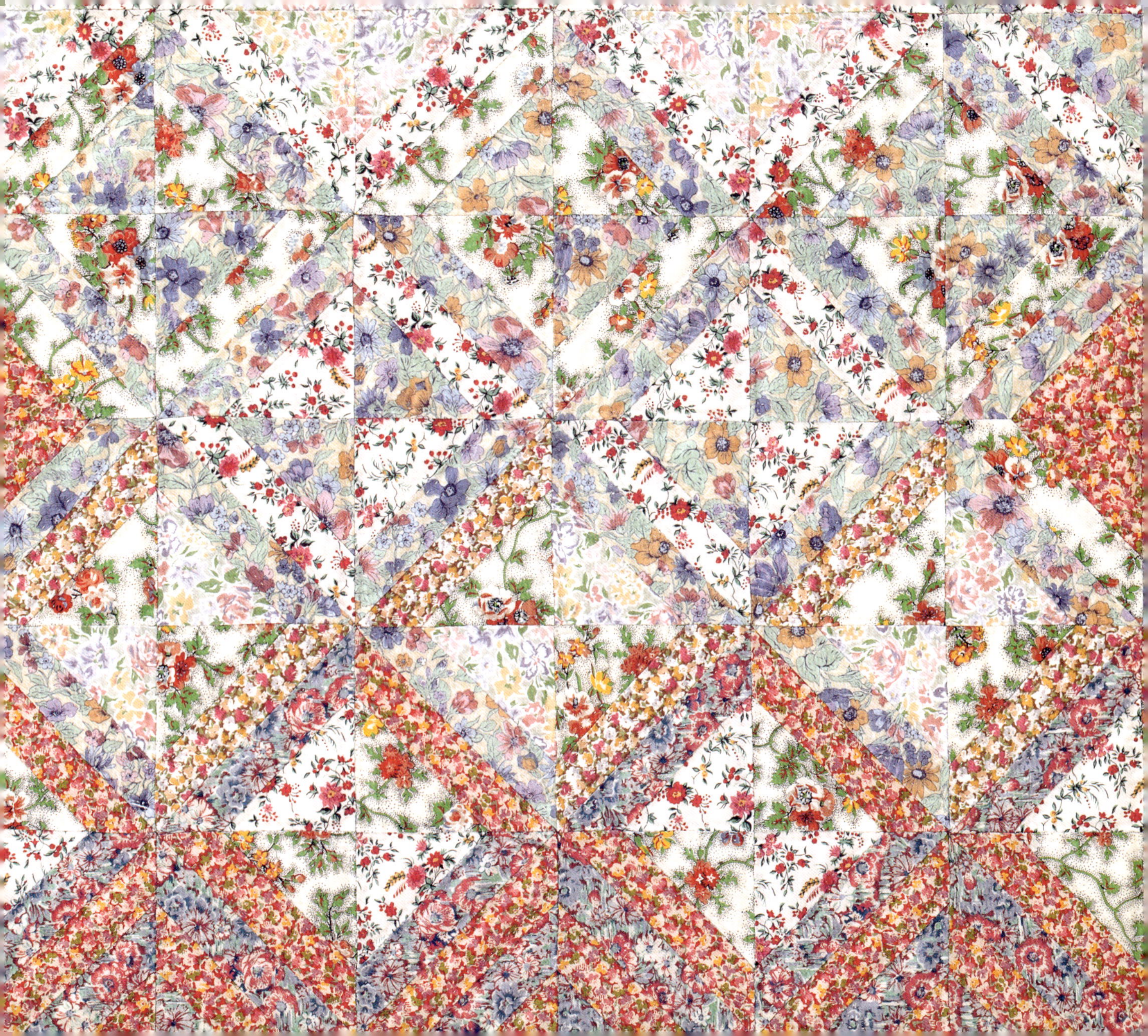

48

10 うさぎのいる風景／Scene with Rabbits

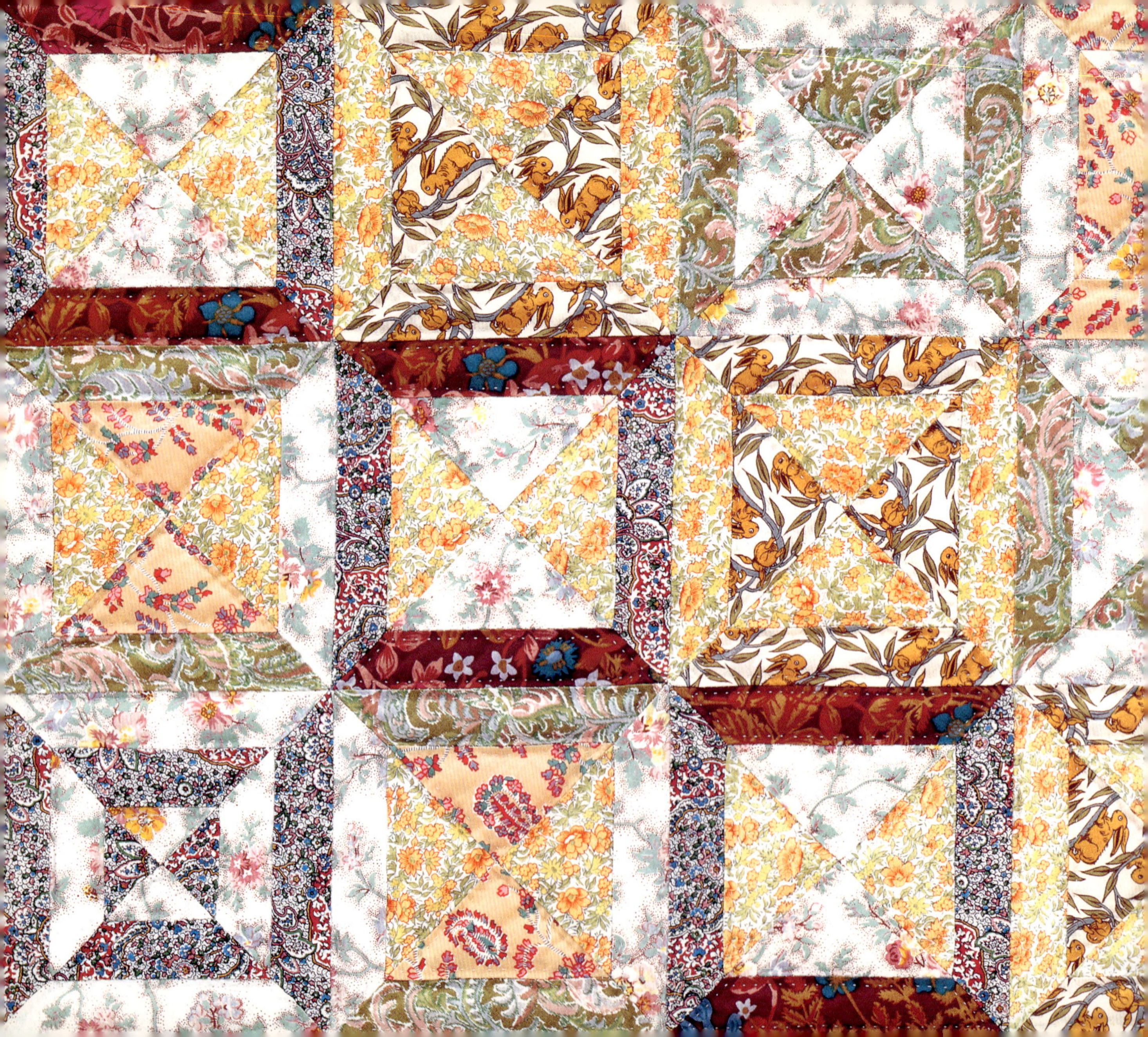

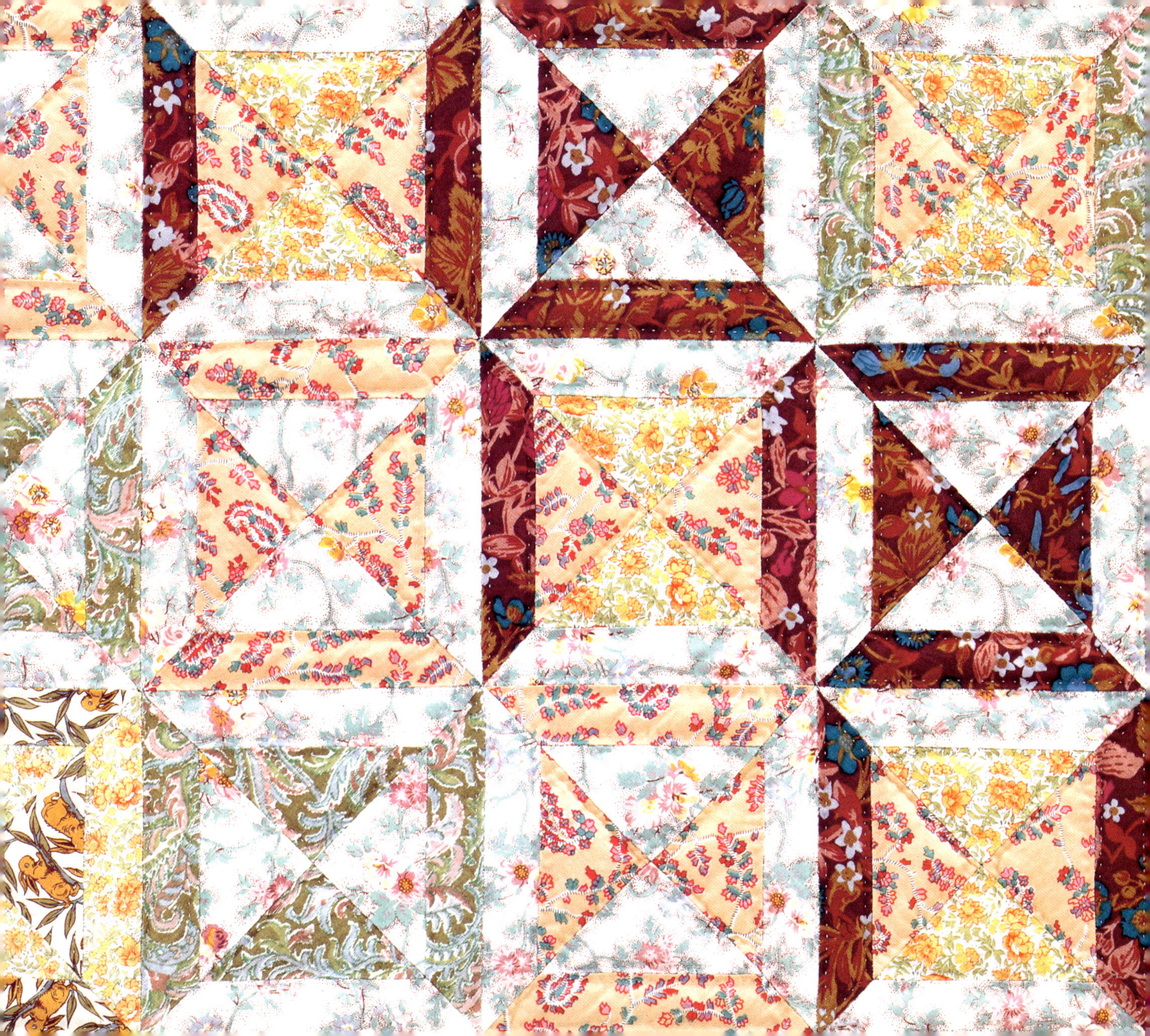

52

11 朝もやの庭／Garden in Morning Mist

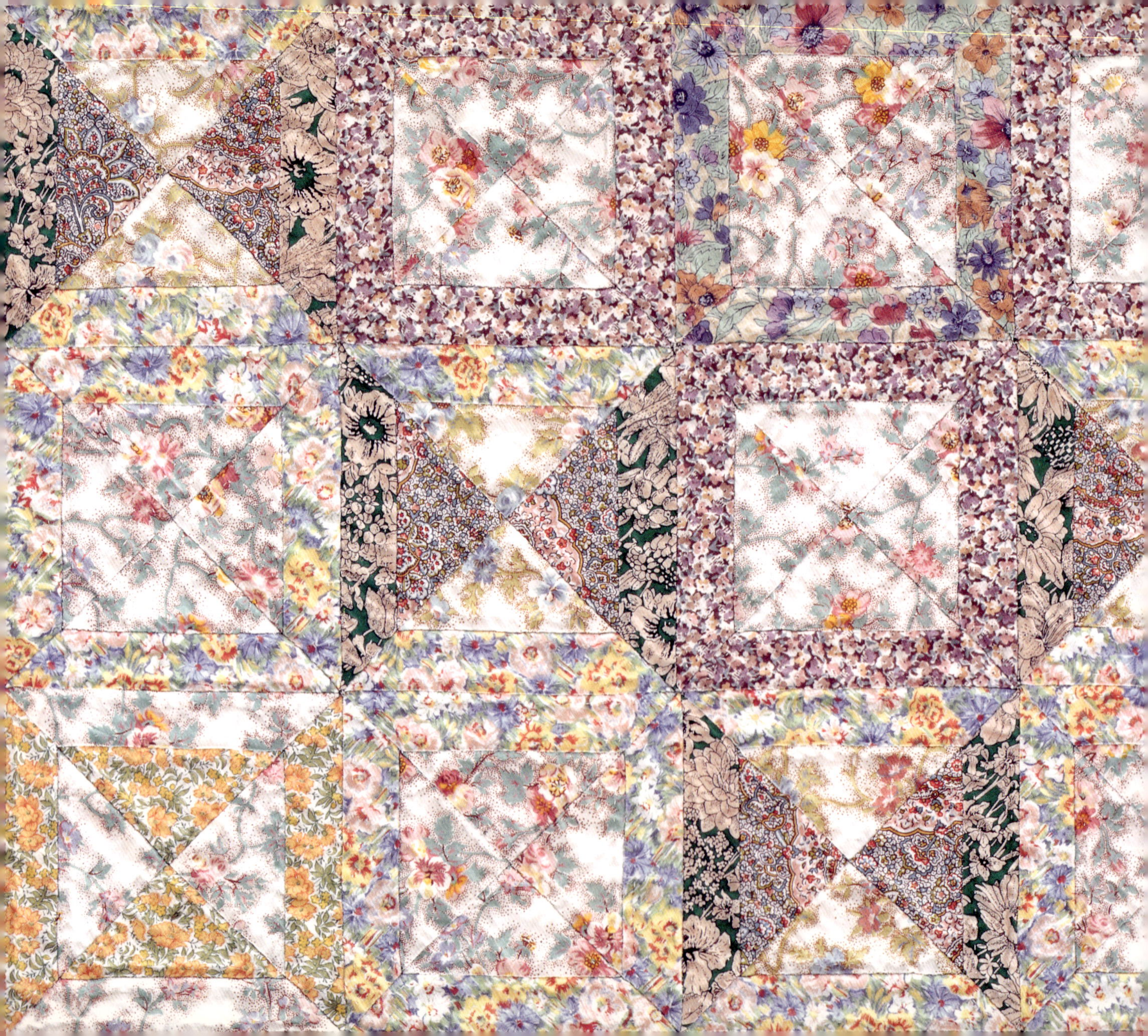

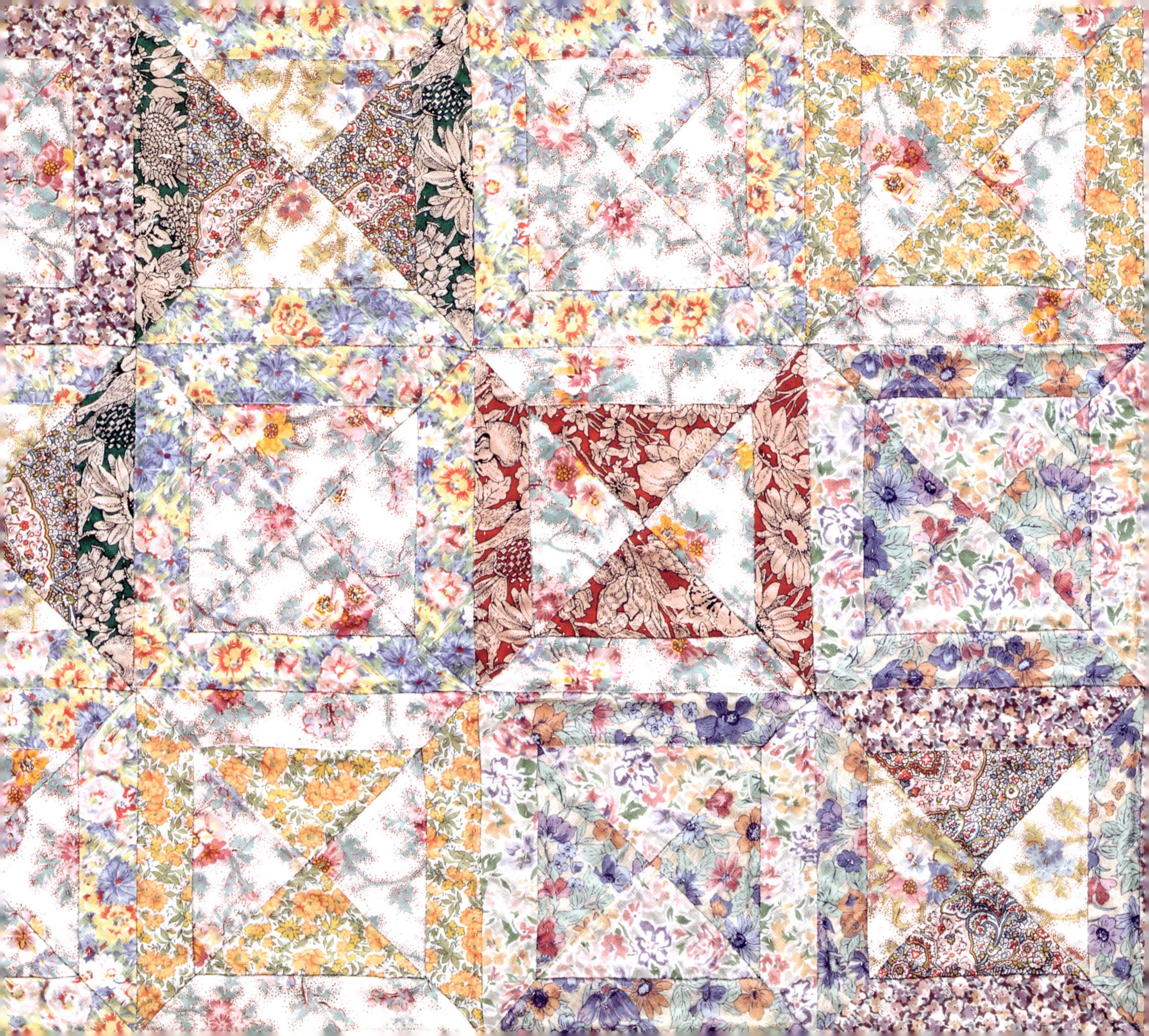

12 春／Spring

13 秋／Autumn

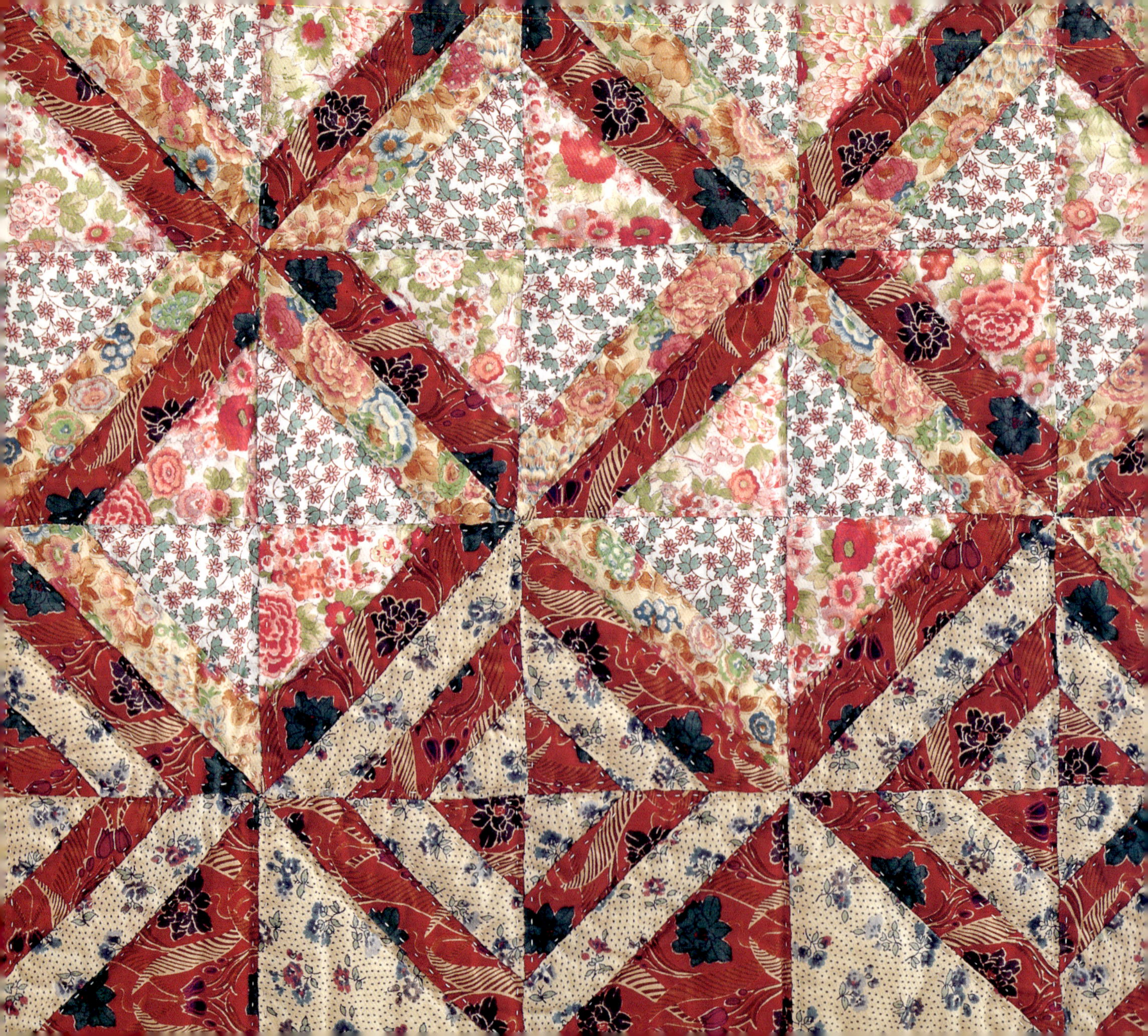

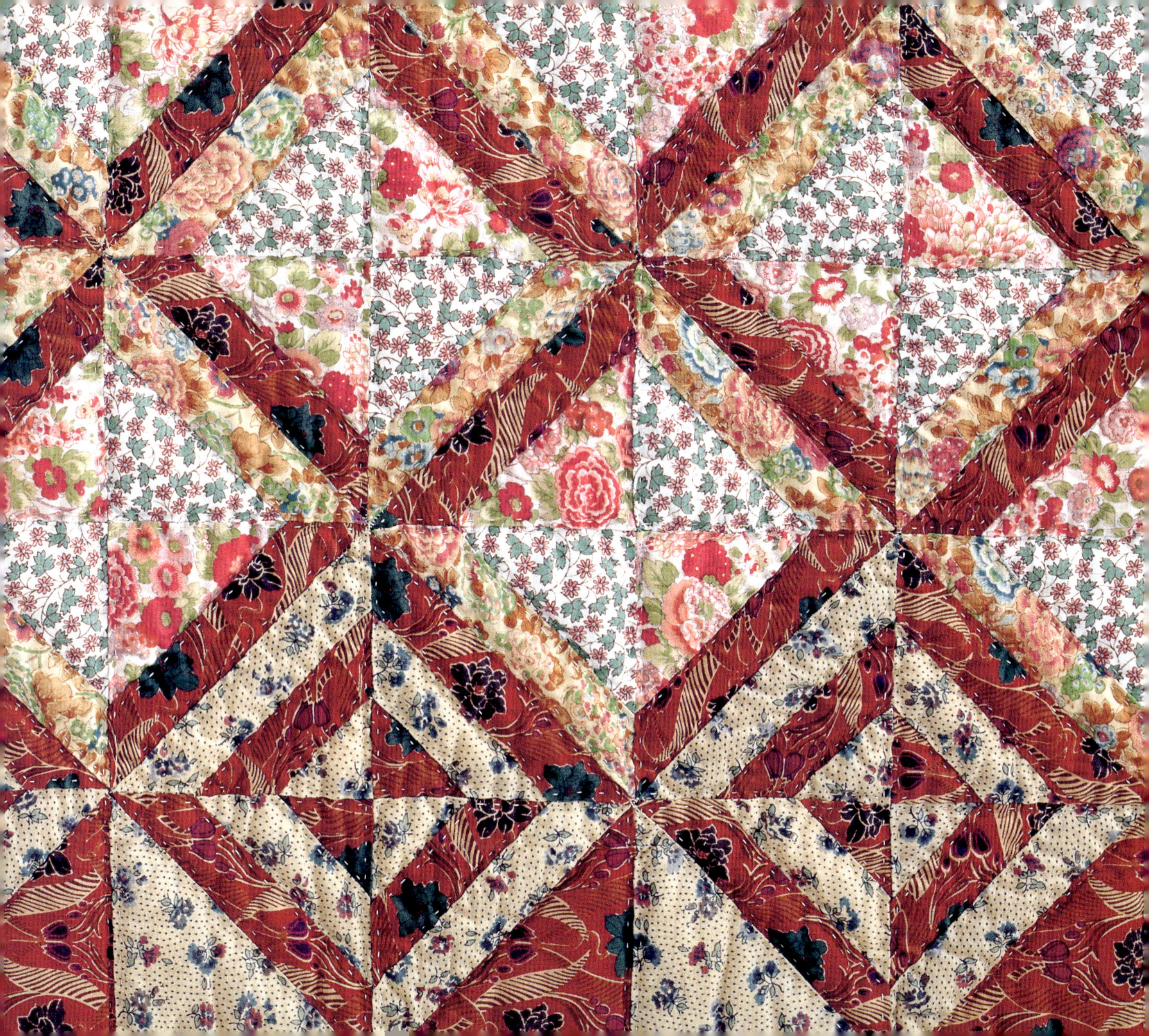

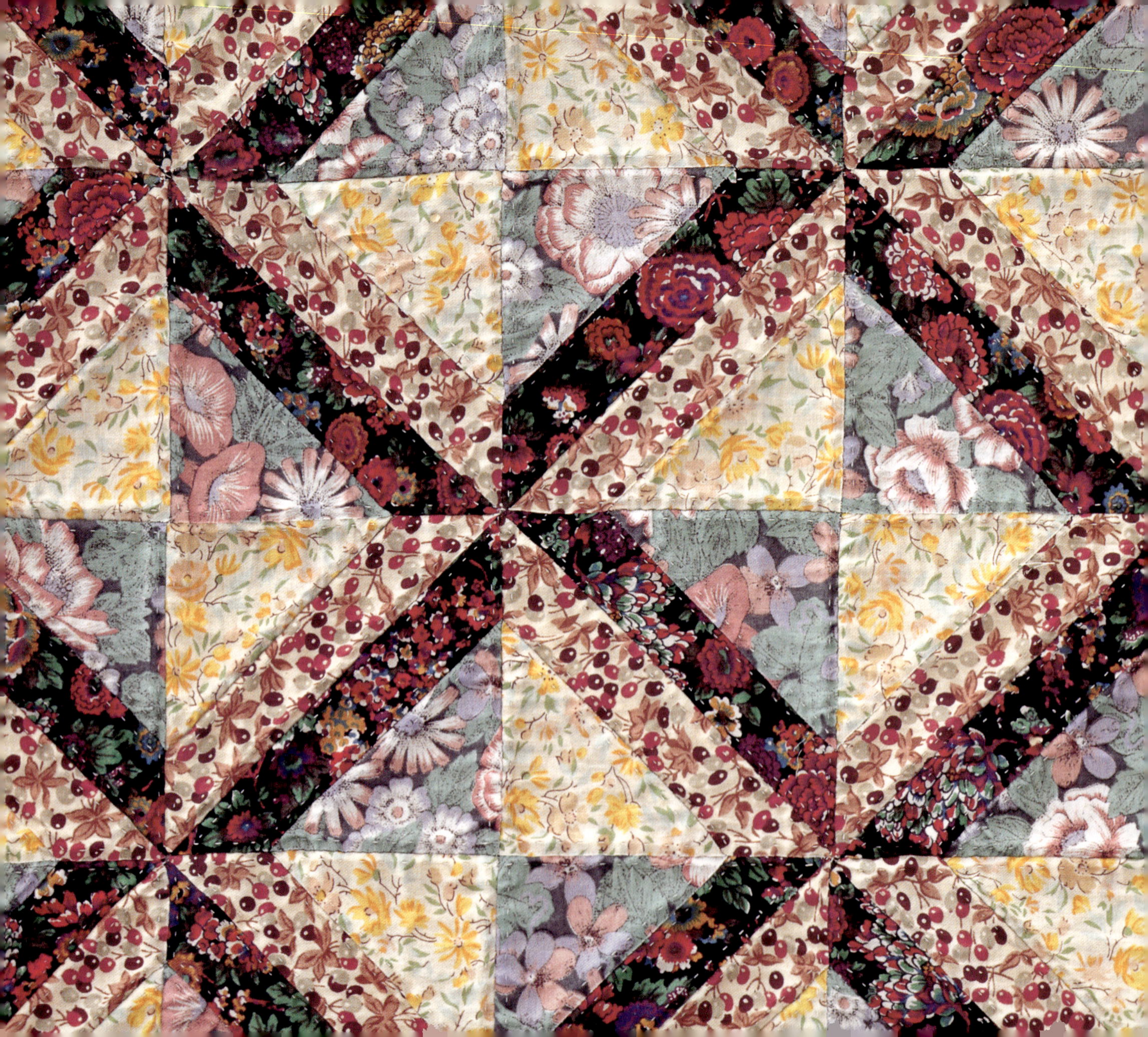

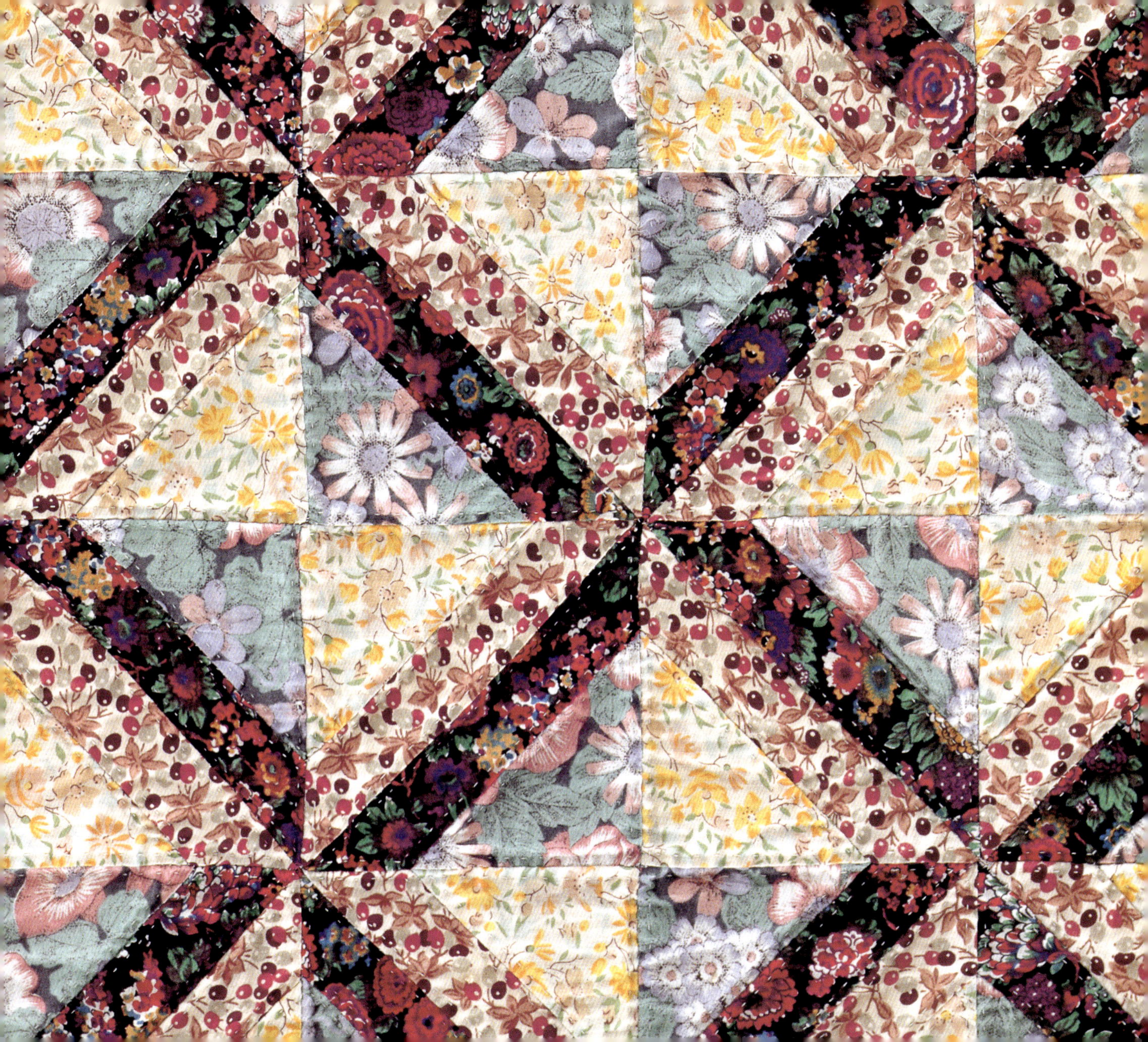

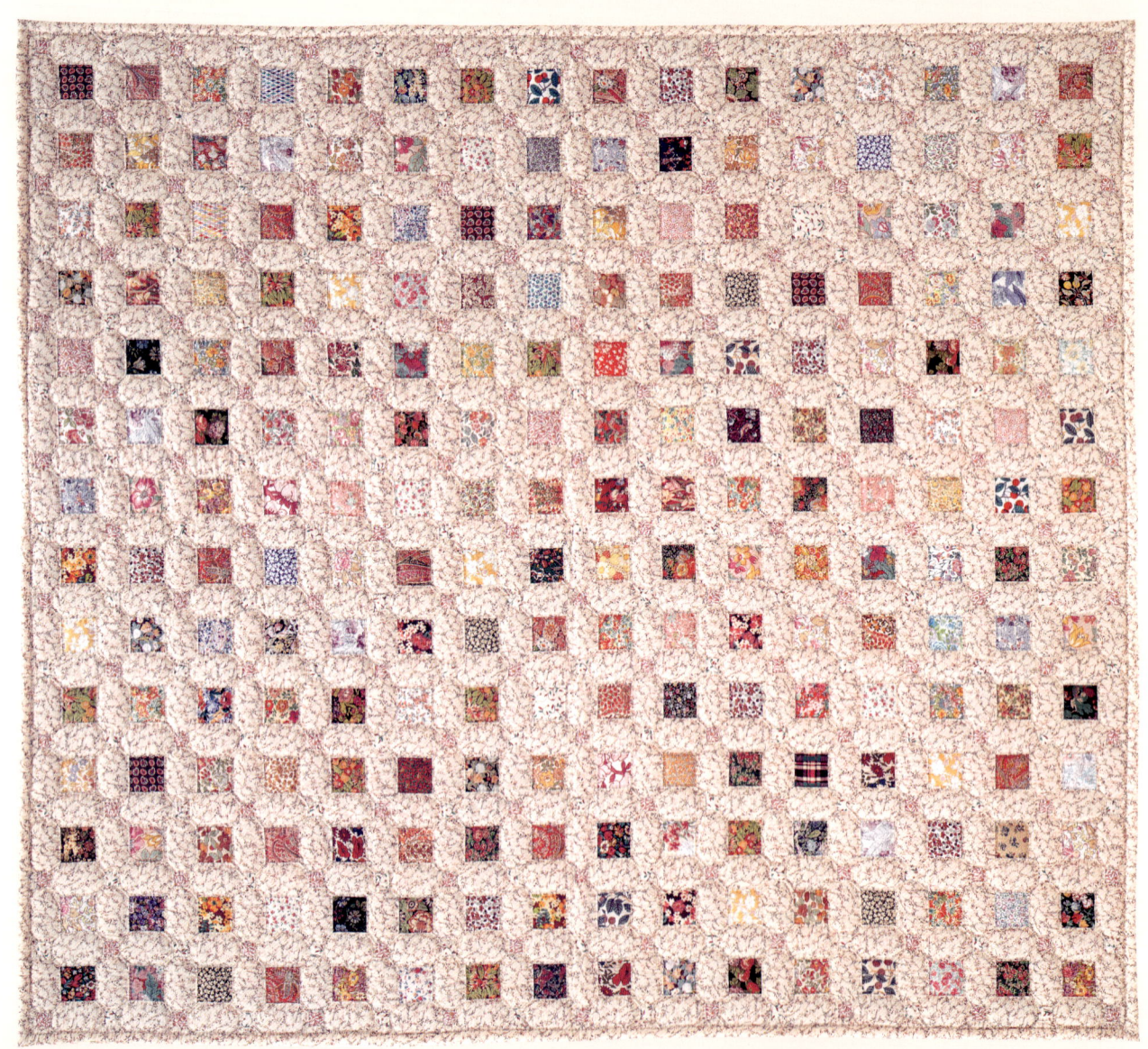

14 センチメンタル・リバティ／Sentimental Liberty

15 センチメンタル・リバティ／Sentimental Liberty

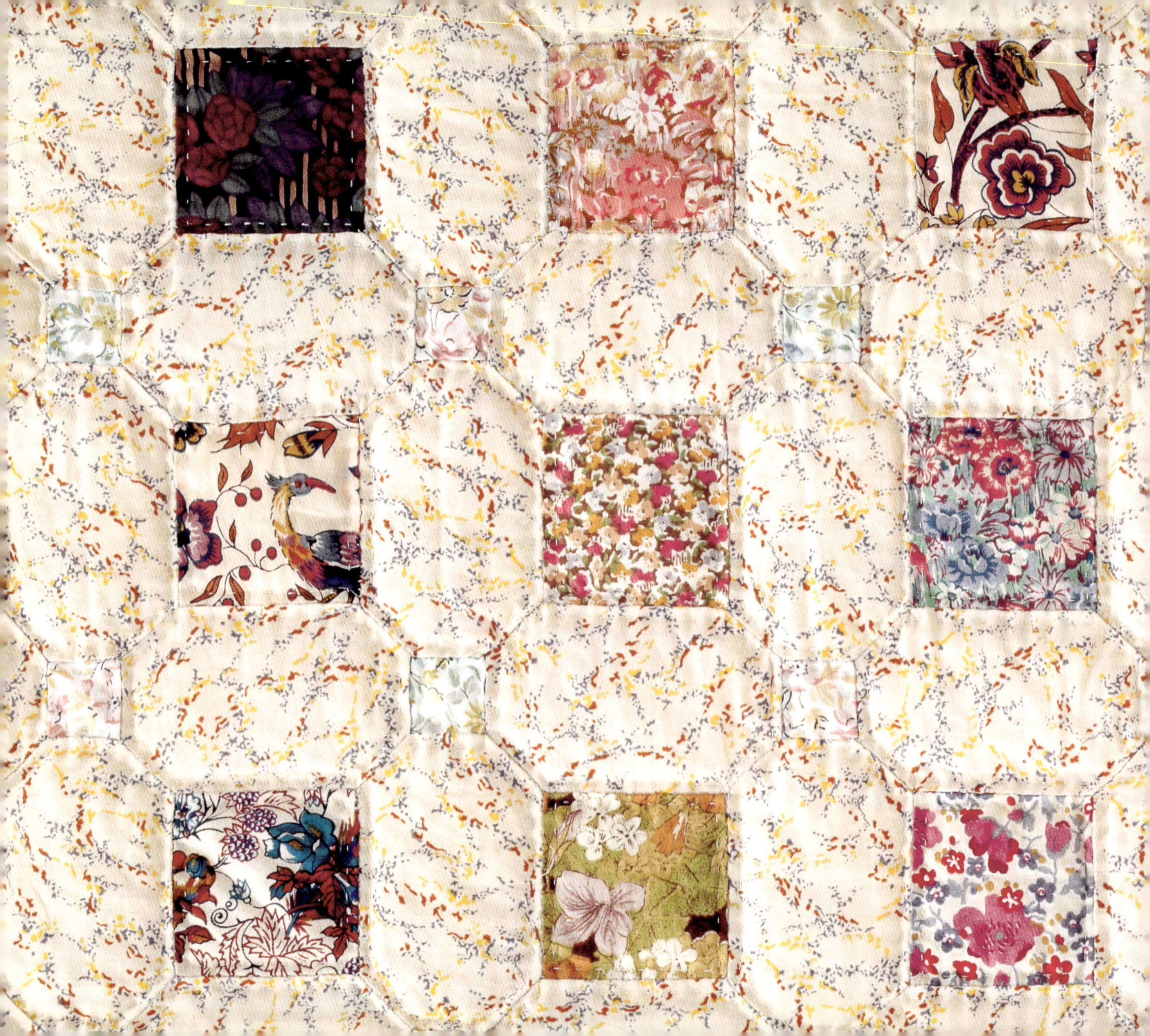

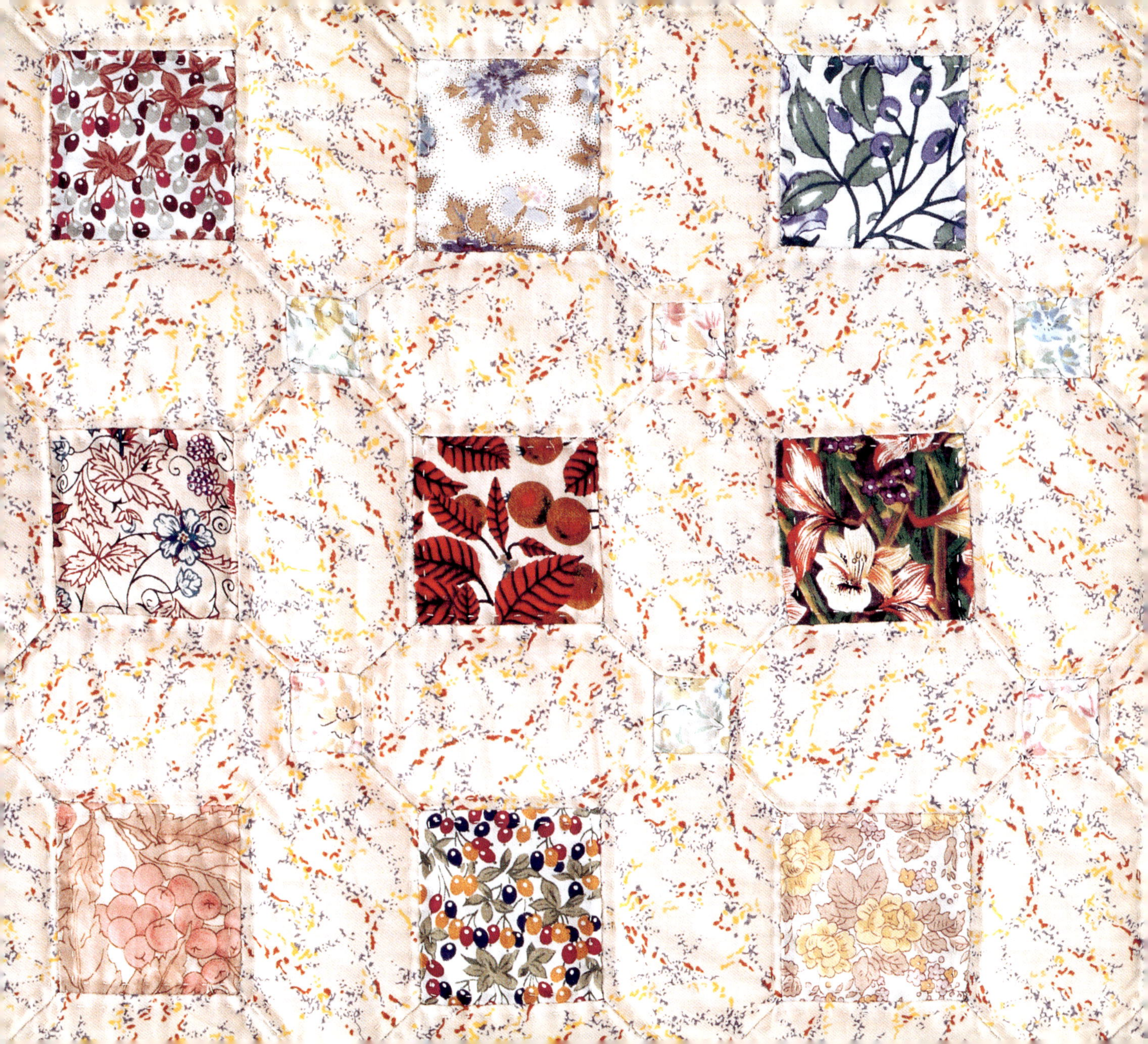

66

16 飾りのついたキルト／Quilt with Flowing Edges

68

17 飾りのついたキルト／Quilt with Flowing Edges

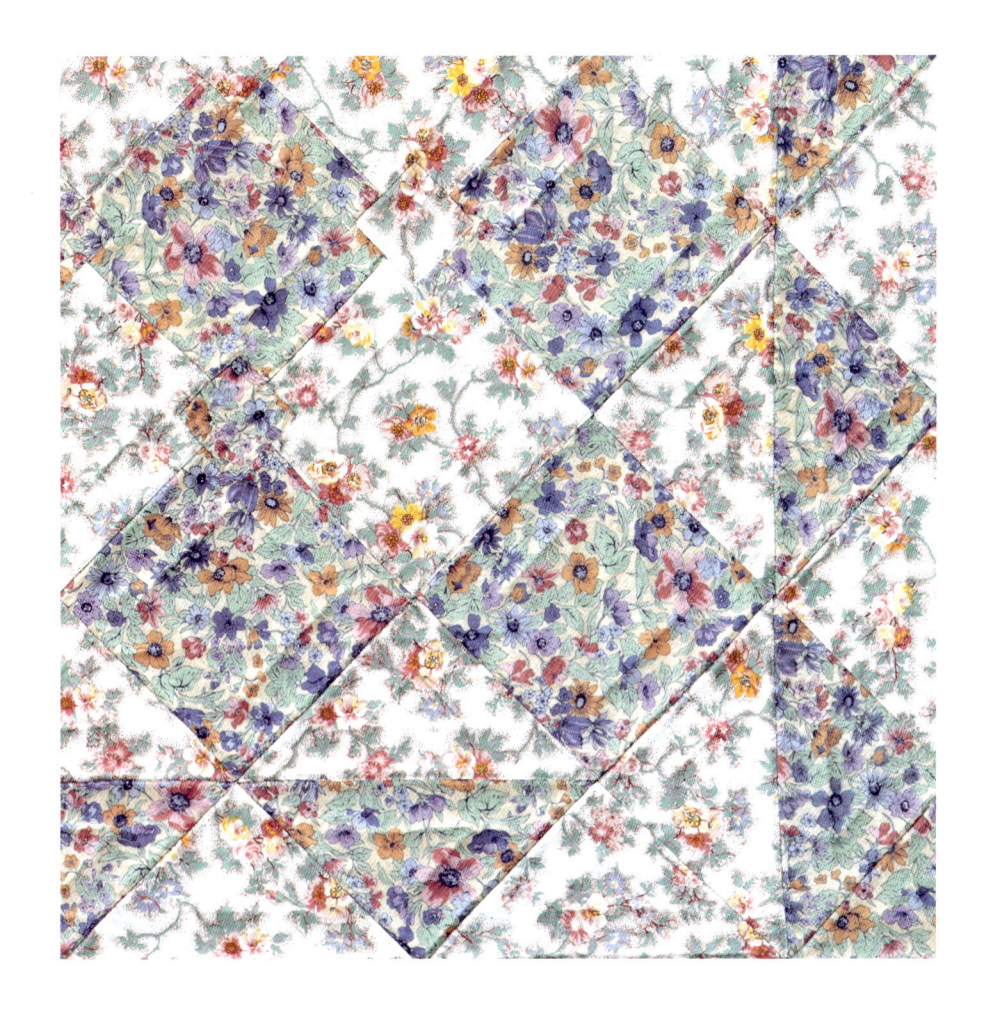

18 リバティ・パレード／Liberty Parade

71

72

73

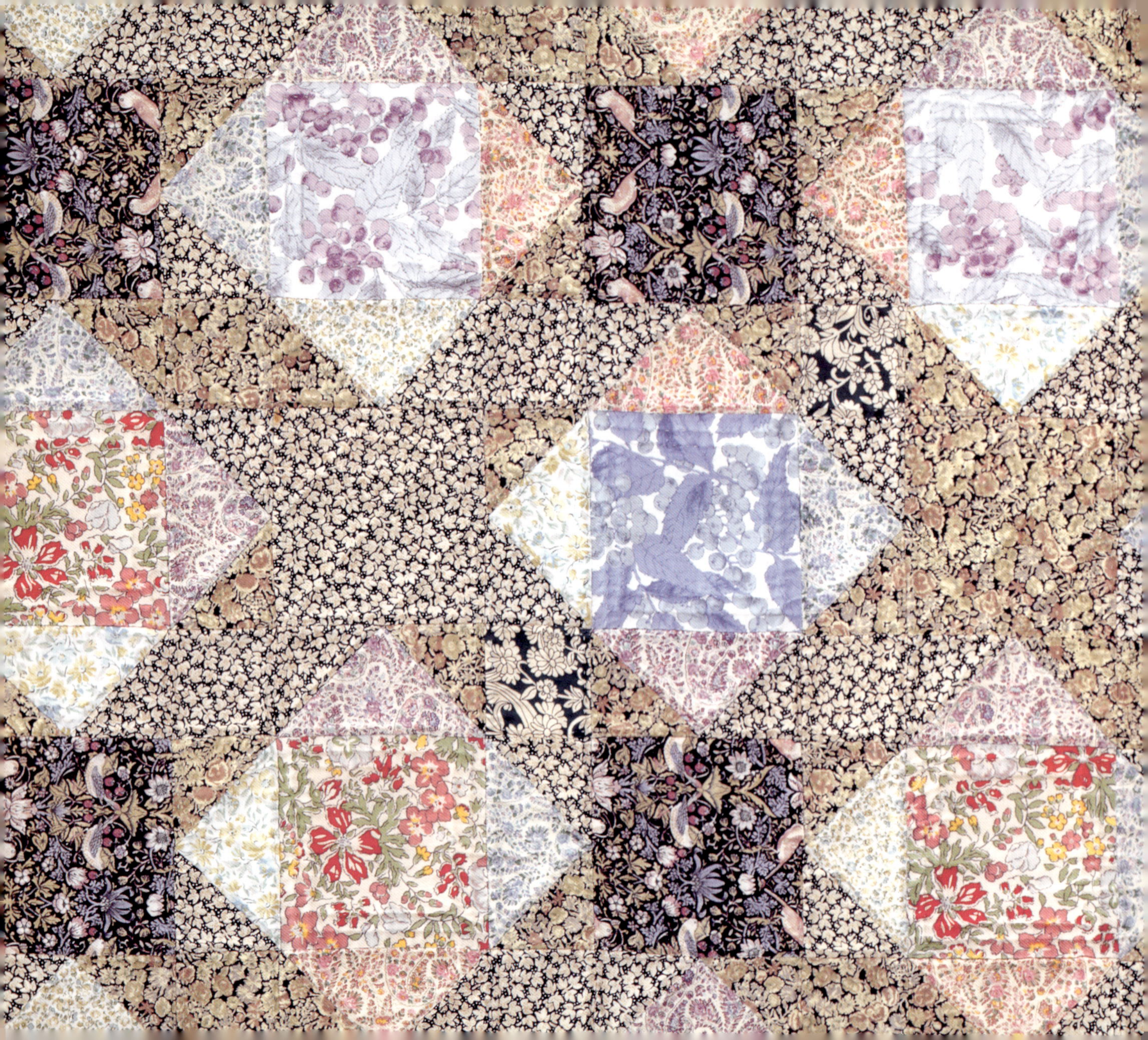

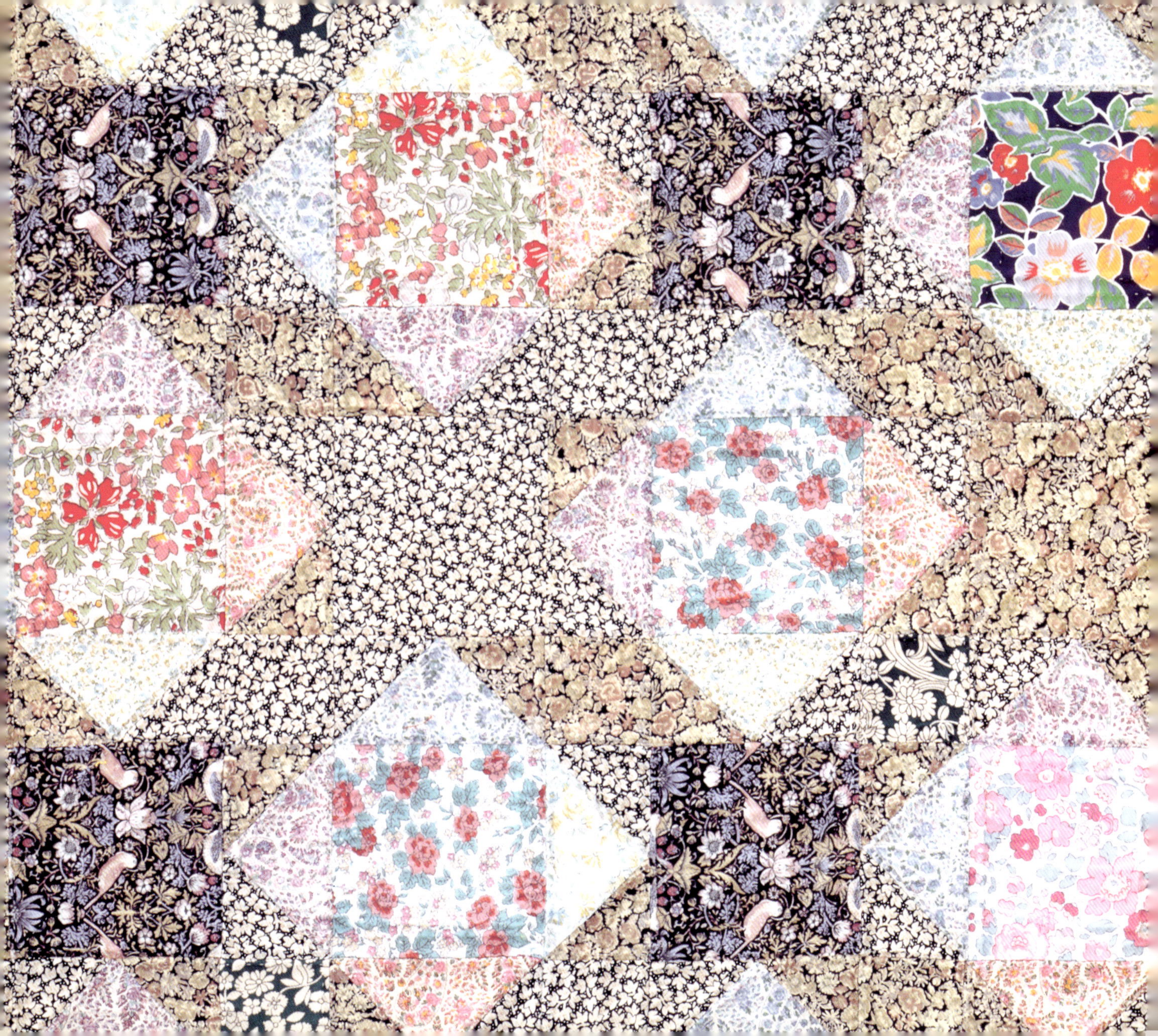

19 紅いダイヤモンド・ダスト／Crimson Diamond Dust

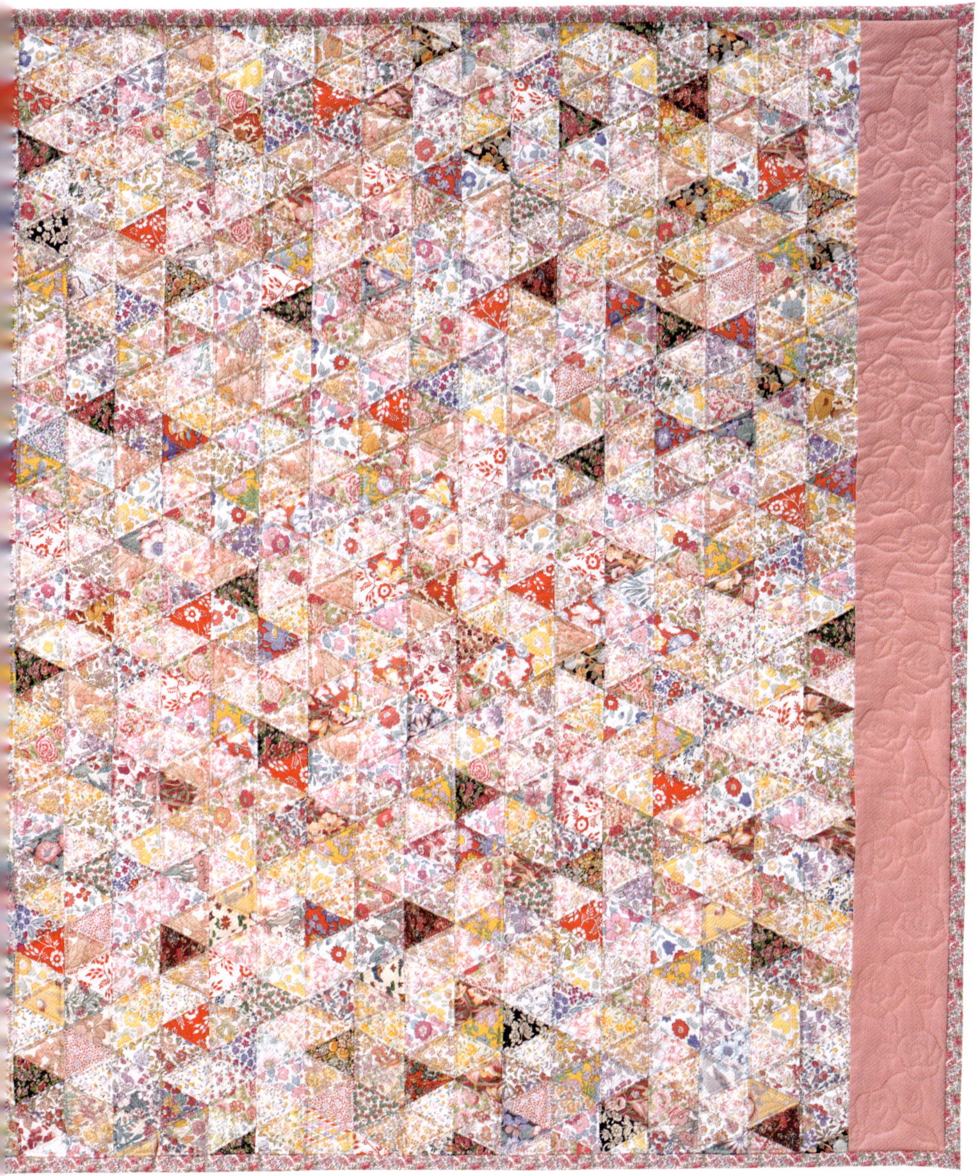

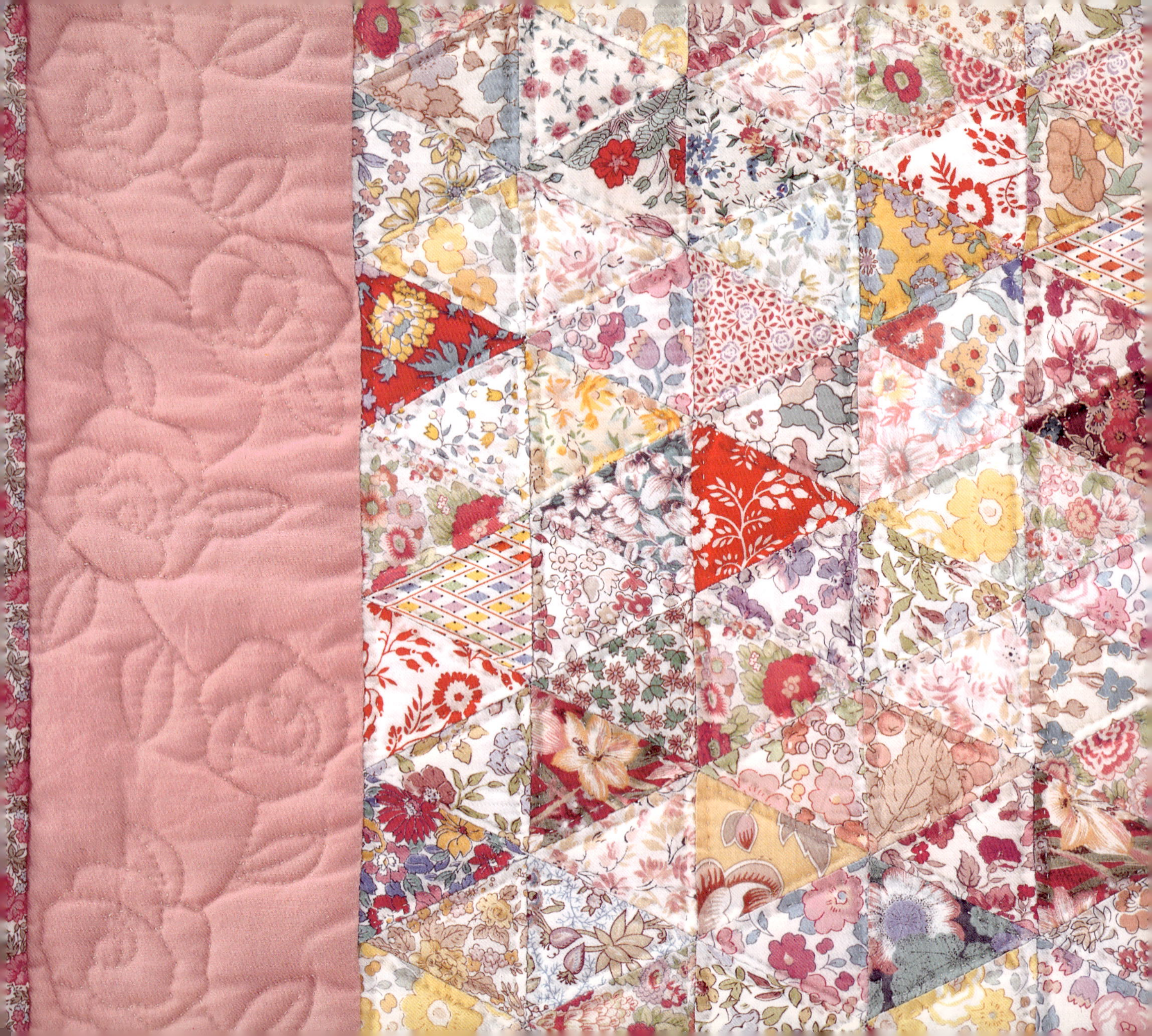

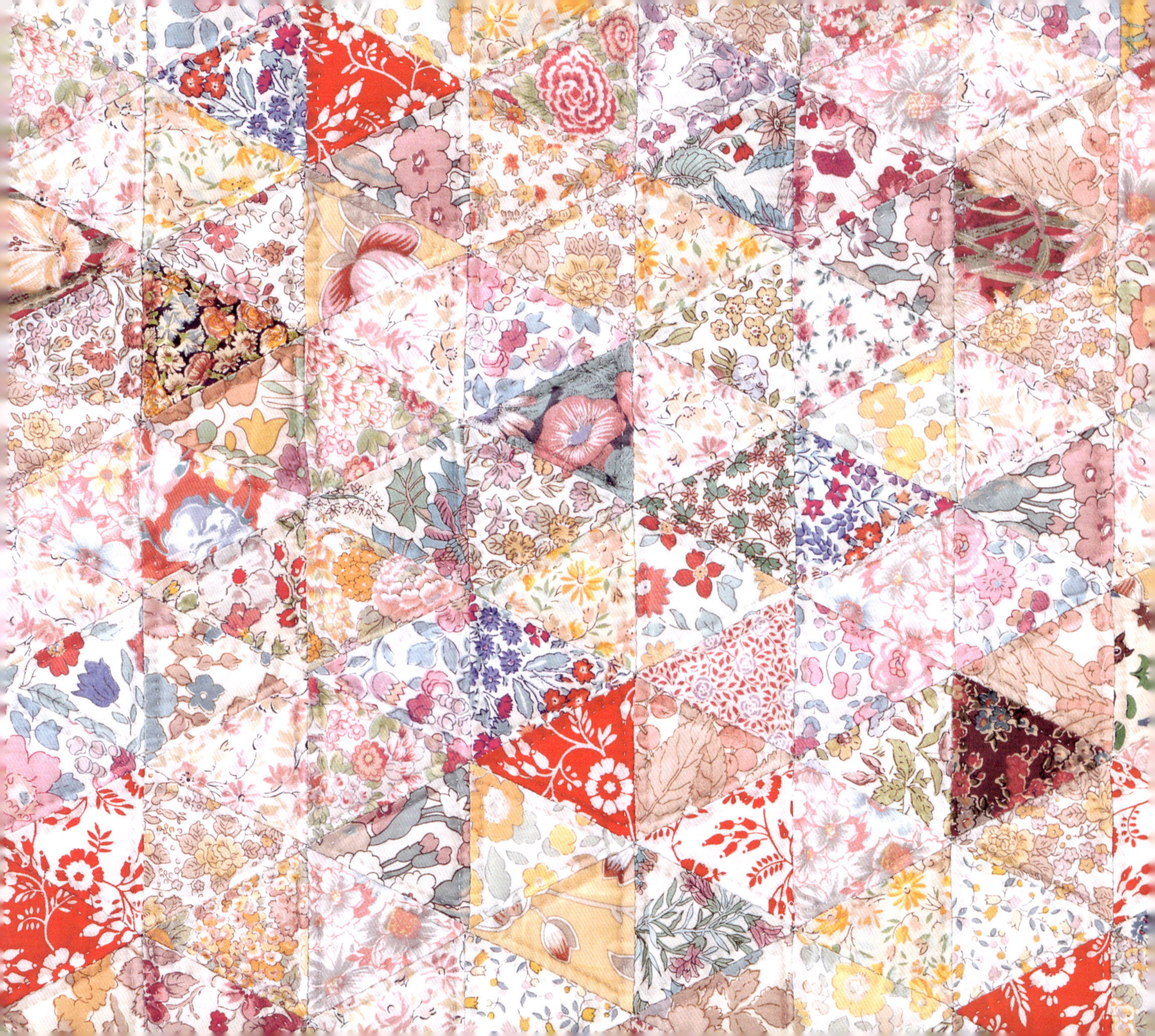

80

20　イエロー・ワルツ／Liberty Waltz

81

82

83

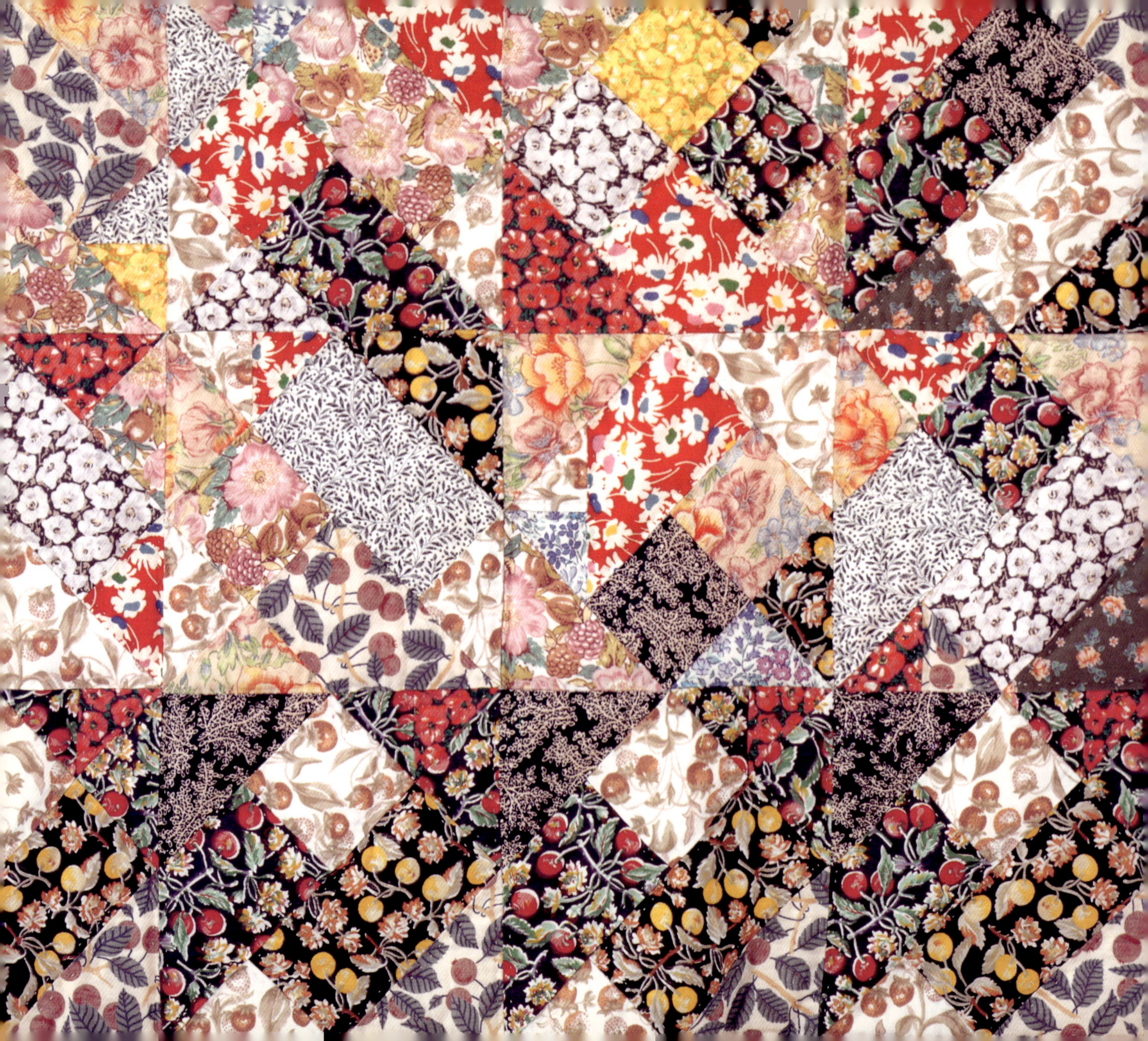

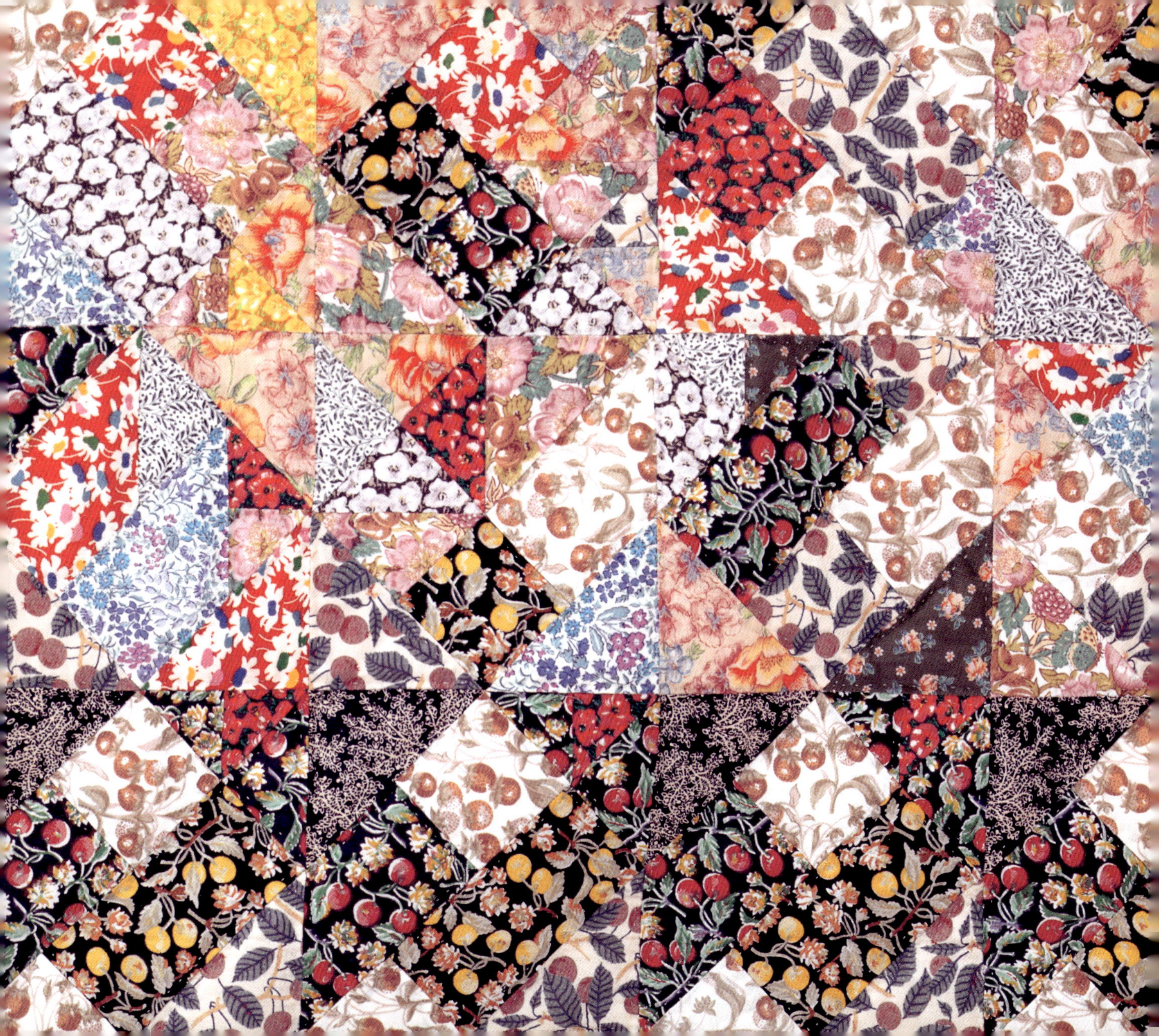

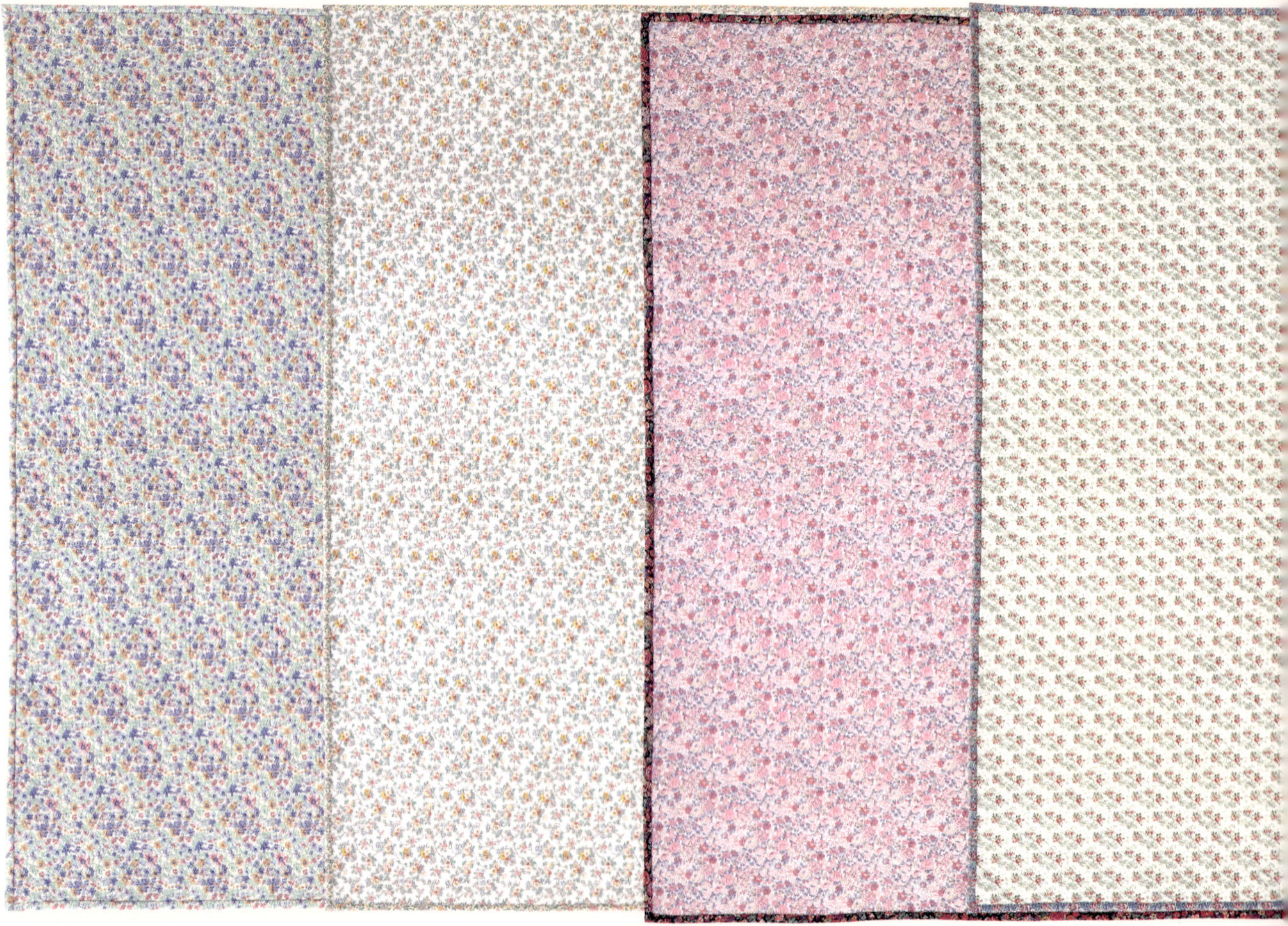

87

藤田治彦
京都工芸繊維大学工芸学部
造形工学科助教授

リバティ・スタイルとフリー・スタイル

PHOETAS〔フィータス〕

アール・ヌーヴォー

　19世紀末から20世紀初頭にかけて、新しい装飾の様式がフランスとベルギーを中心にヨーロッパ全土に広まった。有機的な曲線をもっとも顕著な特色とするこの様式には、その形態上の特徴から「波の様式」や「花の様式」、あるいはそれが使われたもっとも目立つ場所であるパリの地下鉄から「メトロ様式」など、さまざまな名称が与えられた。だが、最終的には今日もなお使われている「アール・ヌーヴォー Art Nouveau」という名前が残った。
　それはドイツ語圏では「ユーゲントシュティル Jugendstil」と呼ばれた。「アール・ヌーヴォー」が「新しい芸術」であるように「ユーゲントシュティル」も「若い様式」を意味しており、ともに過去の諸様式から自らを開放した新しい装飾芸術にふさわしい名称であった。これらの様式名はその流行に関わった店や雑誌の名に由来するものであった。1895年にパリのプロヴァンス街に開店した「メゾン・ド・ラール・ヌーヴォー Maison de L'Art Nouveau」であり、翌1896年にミュンヘンで創刊された「ユーゲント Jugend」である。
　イタリアでは「アール・ヌーヴォー」はフランスよりもむしろイギリスと強く結び付けられていたようで、英国様式「スティーレ・イングレーゼ Stile Inglese」あるいは「スティーレ・リベィルティ Stile Liberty」と呼ばれた。このリベィルティとはロンドンのリバティ商会（百貨店）のことである。

リバティ商会と東洋

　リバティ商会の創設は1875年にさかのぼる。創業者アーサー・リバティはロンドンの北西、バッキンガムシャーのチルタン丘陵の小さな市場町チェシャムで服地商を営む同名の父のもとに1843年に生まれた。後の詩人でテキスタイル・デザインにも多くの優れた作品を残した工芸家、そして社会運動家でもあったウィリアム・モリスがロンドンの北東ウォルサムストウで生まれた9年後のことであった。以下モリスとの比較を交えながら話を進めよう。

　リバティはワイン商を営むおじを頼って16歳でロンドンへ出た。アール・ヌーヴォーの源泉となったイギリスのアーツ・アンド・クラフツ運動の発祥の地ともいえるモリスの「赤い家」建設のころのことである。リバティはワイン店の店員とある服地商の見習いを経て、1862年に最高級の店が並ぶリージェント・ストリートのショールと外套の専門店、ファーマー＆ロジャーズ商会に就職した。

　リバティがその高級店に就職したのはロンドン西郊のケンジントンで万国博覧会が開催された年であった。そこにはイギリスの代表的なゴシック・リヴァイヴァルの建築家たちによる作品に混じって、モリスらが設立した室内装飾事務所兼工房、モリス・マーシャル・フォークナー商会の作品も初めて展示されていた。しかし、リバティがもっとも興味を持ったのは初代駐日英国総領事ラザフォード・オルコックのコレクションを中心とする日本の工芸品の展示であった。

　博覧会終了後、ファーマー＆ロジャーズ商会は日本の工芸品のいくつかを買い取り、本店の隣に設けた東洋物品店の目玉とした。日本の工芸品は日本開国直後の1854年にもロンドンで展示され、そのいくつかを現在のヴィクトリア＆アルバート美術館の前身が購入したようだが、多くの人の目に触れ、広く一般市民の購入の対象となったのはこれが初めてであった。リバティはその東洋物品店の店長を十年以上勤め、それをファーマー＆ロジャーズ商会でもっとも高収益の部門に成長させた。1875年にリバティが独立して同じリージェント・ストリートに自分の店を出すと、芸術家を中心とする顧客もそちらへ移り、ファーマー＆ロジャーズ商会はクリノリンの張り入りスカートの流行の終わりとともに閉店した（商会の主要商品であったショールはスカートの膨らみ具合と社運をともにしたのである）。

　リバティの新しい店は「イースト・インディア・ハウス」と名付けられていたように、日本製品だけを扱う店ではなかった。その初期の取り扱い製品のほとんどは東洋の絹の染め物で、芸術関係者を中心に需要は大きく、その店頭で精妙なあるいは素朴な色で珍しいパターンを染め出した絹布を手に激賞する人々のなかにはモリスの姿もあったという。1860年代から70年代にかけて、イギリス人の趣味とそれを取り巻く商環境は大きく変化した。モリスが内容の劣悪さを察知して入場しなかったという世界初1851年の万国博覧会の逸話、市場にはよい製品がまっ

STRAWBERRY THIEF
ストロベリーシーフ

ウィリアム・モリスのデザインによるリバティ・テキスタイル。
Liberty Textile
Designed by William Morris

たく見つからないので家具を含む室内装飾をすべて自分たちで制作し、それがアーツ・アンド・クラフツ運動の始まりとなったという「赤い家」の逸話は、ある意味ではすでに昔話となっていた。リバティ商会創設の1875年にモリスはモリス・マーシャル・フォークナー商会の権利を完全に独占し、モリス商会として再出発させている。モリスとリバティとのあいだには交流もあったが、それ以上にライバルであった。

リバティ・スタイルとフリー・スタイル

　モリスと異なり、リバティはデザイナーではなかったが、ものを見る目には非凡なものがあった。それは彼が勤務した店での経験の結果だけではなく、下積みのころから演劇界などに親しみ、積極的に深めた芸術家たちとの交友の成果でもあった。リバティ商会に協力した建築家のひとりにE・W・ゴドウィンがいた。ゴドウィンは住宅設計から舞台デザインまでをこなす代表的な日本趣味のデザイナーであった。彼の親友であった建築家ウィリアム・バージェスも、彼がその自邸を設計した画家ホイッスラーも当時の日本趣味の代表的人物であった。また、日本を訪れたことのあるデザイナー、クリストファー・ドレッサーも親しい友人であった。しかし、イタリアで、そして一時はフランスでも「リバティー様式」と呼ばれたものは日本的な様式ではない。もし日本趣味の産物でしかなかったならば、それは「日本様式」と呼ばれたであろう。19世紀イギリスのひとつのスタイルの形成を染めのテキスタイルを例に振り返ってみよう。

　染めは元来東洋の工芸であった。19世紀前半のヨーロッパにおけるプリント・デザインの混乱は、新しい工芸の導入期の試行錯誤のありさまなのである。東洋から導入され近代ヨーロッパ流の改良が加えられた染色技術に染めの芸術が伴わなかったといってもよい。

19世紀半ばにはイギリスでデザイン改革運動が起こり、陰影を施したまるで絵画のようなプリントや壁紙のデザインに批判が加えられ、独自の平面デザインが追求された。だが、その一方でパターンの自然さは失われ、紋章のような生気のないデザインが広まった。

このような状態において新鮮な刺激を与えたのは確かに日本の意匠であった。それに対する反応には大きく分けてふたつあった。ひとつはモリスのそれである。すでに紹介したように、モリスは日本の意匠を知っていた。だが、彼はむしろそれを刺激にしながらもヨーロッパの伝統上に独自のデザインを生み出そうとした。もうひとつがリバティのそれである。彼はもっと自由であった。率直に、日本をはじめ東洋のテキスタイルを輸入販売した。だからといって、リバティが独自のデザインを生み出さなかったわけではない。事実、彼自身、優雅な「アート・カラー」の開発に代表される染めの技術の改良を指揮するなどアート・ディレクター的な役割を十分に果たし、リバティ様式と呼ばれるようになるデザインの核を形成したのであった。

リバティは世紀末には多数の外部デザイナーを採用して、モリス商会の製品に対抗した。そのなかには、より自由でドメスティックな古典主義の復活であったクイーン・アン復興様式をさらに自由にした住宅の建築家、C・F・A・ヴォイジーらも含まれていた。リバティ製品の魅力はまさにそれらのイギリス人デザイナーによるデザインの魅力である。彼らは次の時代のデザイナーのように伝統も様式も否定しないが、ゴシック復興の時代の人々のようにそれにこだわることもなく、自由であった。「リバティ」は姓であり、その様式名としての流布を、その「自由」という意味がどの程度助けたのかは不明である。だが、「リバティ・スタイル」が「フリー・スタイル」であり、イメージの自由さがその最大の魅力であったことだけは確かである。

協力●リバティ・ジャパン

BURNHAM バーナム

by Haruhiko FUJITA
Kyoto Institute of Technology
Faculty of Engineering and Design
Department Architecture and Design
Assistant Professor

Liberty Style and Free Style

Art Nouveau

At the turn of the 20th century, a new decorative style prevailed all over Europe beginning in France and Belgium. Characterized by organic, undulating lines; various names were given to these new designs such as "Wavy style" and "Floral style" after its specific shapes, and "Metro Style" after the subway station in Paris where this style was most conspicuously displayed. However, the term "Art Nouveau" has outlived all the others.

In German speaking countries the style was called "Jugendstil." Art Nouveau means "new art," whereas this term means "young style," both of which are appropriate names to describe the new decorative art which strived to liberate itself from the traditional styles of the past. "Art Nouveau" and "Jugendstil" were derived respectively from the name of a shop and of a magazine, both of which had close relationships with the movement. The shop was "Maison de L'Art Nouveau" which opened in 1895 on the Rue de Provence, Paris. The magazine was "Jugend," whose initial issue was published in the following year in Munich.

In Italy, this new art movement was associated with the British rather than with the French, and was called "Stile inglese" or "Stile Liberty." This "Liberty" refers to the Liberty Company of London.

The Liberty Company and Asia

The Liberty Company was established in 1875. The founder, Arthur Lasenby Liberty, was born in 1843 in a draper's family in the small Buckinghamshire market town of Chesham northwest of London. Nine years preceding this, William Morris, the poet, political activist and craftsman who was also known for his excellent textile designs, was born in Walthamstow, northeast of London.

When Arthur Liberty was sixteen, he moved to London to work with his uncle, who was a wine dealer. It was about the same time that Morris's "Red House" was built, which was considered to be the birthplace of the Arts and Crafts Movement. Liberty worked as a clerk in his uncle's shop, then became an apprentice to a draper for two years before getting a position in 1862 at Farmer & Rogers, an establishment specializing in shawls and cloaks in Regent Street where the high-quality shops of London were concentrated.

In the same year that Liberty was hired by this exclusive shop, the second London International Exhibition was held in Kensington, west of the city. Among the works by representative English Gothic

Revival architects, the products of Morris, Marshall, Faulkner & Co. were exhibited for the first time to the public. This firm was virtually a combination office-workshop for interior decoration made by Morris and his friends. However, what Liberty was most attracted to was the display of Japanese crafts which consisted primarily of the collection of Rutherford Alcock, the first British Consul General to Japan.

After the exhibition, Farmer and Rogers bought some pieces from the Japanese exhibit and made them the chief attraction for their new shop, Oriental Warehouse, which opened on premises adjacent to the main shop. Eight years prior to this exhibition, in 1854, some Japanese artifacts had been displayed for the first time in London when Japan opened its doors to the West by reversing its national seclusion policy. Some of the articles displayed were said to have been purchased by the predecessor of the Victoria & Albert Museum. Nevertheless, the 1862 exhibition was the first time that Japanese crafts were presented to the public in general.

Arthur Liberty worked for the Oriental Warehouse as a manager for twelve years and made it the most profitable part of the enterprise. In 1875 Arthur Liberty left in order to open his own shop, also on Regent street. As a result, all of his old customers, mostly artists, began to frequent his shop. Farmer & Rogers subsequently closed, as crinoline skirts went out of fashion, the main merchandise of Farmer & Rogers, shawls, also became unpopular. It can be said that Farmer & Rogers shared its fate with the swelling of skirts.

As the name "East India House" indicates, Liberty's new shop didn't handle only articles from Japan. During its early days, the main merchandise was dyed silk from the East, which were in high demand by the customers, especially who were related to art. Among the people in the shop who praised the silk fabric dyed in subtle and natural colours, was William Morris. From the 1860s to the 1870s, the aesthetic tastes of the British people and the surrounding business environment had changed substantially. The earlier anecdotes about William Morris, that he did not go into the first International Exhibition in 1851 because he felt its quality inferior or that at his "Red House" he set out to design and make his own interior decorations (including furniture) out of disappointment with contemporary design, and that it was this that led to the Arts and Crafts Movement: were things of the past. In 1875 when Liberty opened his shop, Morris obtained exclusive ownership of Morris, Marshall, Faulkner & Co., and restarted it as Morris & Co. Although Liberty and Morris had some connections, they were rivals rather than friends.

Liberty style and free style

Unlike Morris, Liberty was not a designer, but he did have an amazingly discerning eye, gained through his experience of working in the design shop as well as his natural inclination to all forms of art including the theatre, and the wide and deep association with artists which he had pursued since his early days. One of the architects who collaborated with Liberty Co. was E. W. Godwin, a representative architect of the "Japanism" style, who designed a full range of architecture from houses to theatre stages. His close friend, William Burges, also an architect, and the painter Whistler, whose house Burges designed, were also known as artists of the "Japanism" style. Christopher Dresser, a designer who had actually visited Japan, was also a good friend of Liberty's. This style, which was called "Liberty Style" in Italy and for a brief time in France, was not synonymous with real Japanese style. If this style was merely a product of the "Japanism" style, it should have been called "Japanese Style."

I want to review how one art style evolved in Britain, taking the development of dyed textiles as an example.

Dyeing was originally an Asian craft. The confusion seen in print design in early 19th century Europe illustrates the typical trial-and-error stage of an introductory period. Artistic skill had not matured enough to fully utilize the dyeing techniques which had been brought from the East and improved on by modern European science.

Around the mid 19th century, a revolution took place in overall design in Britain; much criticism was directed at the patterns of printed fabrics and wallpapers, which looked just like paintings with shading, so the opportunity to create independent, original designs became an increasingly important part of the design world. However, on the other hand, the naturalness or liveliness which one could see in the old designs was lost, to be replaced by lifeless, conventional designs resembling crest motifs.

Under such circumstances, Japanese designs with their fresh images certainly provided not a little stimulation to the art world. There are two recognized types of reactions toward Japanese art: one that of Morris and the other that of Liberty. As was mentioned before, Morris was familiar with Japanese design. Using these as a stimulus, he tried to create unique designs of his own as an extension of European tradition. On the other hand, Liberty's attitude was more free; he simply imported textiles from Japan and other countries in the East and sold them. That does not mean he did not create any designs of his own. As a matter of fact, he played an important role as an art director or producer in terms of improving dyeing techniques, including the invention of his own elegant "Art Colours," and his success in forming the nucleus of the "Liberty Style."

At the end of the century, Liberty hired many designers from outside the company to compete with the products of Morris & Co. Among them was C. F. A. Voysey, an architect known for his unique houses which further developed the free, domestic style of "Queen Anne Revival." The allure of Liberty's products, in itself, is that of the designs produced by these British designers. They did not deny traditional styles, like designers of the following generation, nor did they stick to them as the Gothic Revival designers did. They were free of conventions. It is not clear how much advantage the family name "Liberty" had in diffusing the name of the style itself. However, it is certain that "Liberty Style" was a "Free Style" and the freedom shown in design was the most characteristic property of Liberty.

List

1	アルハンブラの思い出	Memory of Alhambra	155×155cm
2	アルハンブラの思い出	Memory of Alhambra	183×228cm
3	プロヴァンスのキルト	Provençal Quilt	174×234cm
4	パイルドキルト	Piled Quilt	177×217cm
5	パイルドキルト	Piled Quilt	198×242cm
6	アンドロメダ星雲の夜明け	Dawn of Andromeda	166×164cm
7	モノクローム・モザイク	Monochromic Mosaic	110×178cm
8	ベルサイユの庭	Garden of Versailles	185×185cm
9	イギリスの庭	Old England Garden	180×180cm
10	うさぎのいる風景	Scene with Rabbits	180×180cm
11	朝もやの庭	Garden in Morning Mist	177×177cm
12	春	Spring	178×178cm
13	秋	Autumn	130×130cm
14	センチメンタル・リバティ	Sentimental Liberty	144×163cm
15	センチメンタル・リバティ	Sentimental Liberty	147×167cm
16	飾りのついたキルト	Quilt with Flowing Edges	157×157cm
17	飾りのついたキルト	Quilt with Flowing Edges	155×155cm
18	リバティ・パレード	Liberty Parade	180×223cm
19	紅いダイヤモンド・ダスト	Crimson Diamond Dust	115×147cm
20	イエロー・ワルツ	Liberty Waltz	185×185cm

作品協力

荒居治子
荒木のぶ子
神田不二世
斉吉桂子
鈴木真子
山本由美子

リバティの詩(うた)
2　ベッドカバー

発行············1994年12月10日
著者············中西一女子
制作者··········安田英樹
発行者··········藤岡　護
発行············株式会社 京都書院
　　　　　　京都市中京区堀川通三条上ル
　　　　　　TEL 075-711-0212　FAX 075-711-0067
制作············漂蒼庵
編集············姫野希美
写真············スタジオ カンノ
翻訳············スタイナー紀美子
デザイン··········南部麻子
印刷製本··········大平印刷株式会社

©1994 by Himeko Nakanishi
ISBN4-7636-3243-4 C5376
Printed in Japan